Reading EGGSPRESS

READING

• Comprehension • Spelling • Grammar • Review

2

Blake e LEARNING

Contents

Year Planner

	Week 1	Week 2	Week 3	Week 4	Week 5	Week 6	Week 7	Week 8	Week 9
Comprehension	Think marks	Finding facts and information	Making inferences	Finding the main idea	Finding the main idea	Finding facts and information	Compare and contrast	Finding the main idea	Sequencing events
Spelling	Verb endings: s, es	Digraphs: ar, or	Endings: y, ey	scr, spr, str	Digraph: qu	Suffixes: ing, ed	Prefix: un	Digraph: oo	Soft c
Grammar	Common nouns	Collective nouns	Proper nouns	Personal pronouns	Articles and nouns	Punctuating statements	Adjectives	Irregular plurals	Commas in letters
Review	Spelling			Grammar			Comprehension		

	Week 10	Week 11	Week 12	Week 13	Week 14	Week 15	Week 16	Week 17	Week 18
Comprehension	Making inferences	Visualization	Finding the main idea	Visualization	Sequencing events	Compare and contrast	Compare and contrast	Making connections	Word study
Spelling	Plurals with y	The j sound	Endings: le, el, al	Digraph: wh	Exceptions	Plurals: s, ves	Long oo exceptions	Suffixes: ful, less	Silent letters
Grammar	Action verbs	Simple present and past tense	Periods and question marks	Linking verbs	Auxiliary verbs	Progressive tense	Future tense	Reflexive pronouns	Periods and exclamation points
Review	Spelling			Grammar			Comprehension		

	Week 19	Week 20	Week 21	Week 22	Week 23	Week 24	Week 25	Week 26	Week 27
Comprehension	Think marks	Making inferences	Visualization	Finding the main idea	Finding the main idea	Sequencing events	Finding facts and information	Compare and contrast	Making inferences
Spelling	Suffixes: er, est	Homophones	Suffixes: ing, ed	The k sound: k, ck	Suffix: ly	Endings: dge, ge	Compound words	Contractions	Plurals: s, es
Grammar	Possessive nouns	Possessive pronouns	Saying verbs	Direct speech	Adverbs of manner	Adverbs of time	Noun phrases	Adjectives and adverbs	Contractions
Review	Spelling			Grammar			Comprehension		

	Week 28	Week 29	Week 30	Week 31	Week 32	Week 33	Week 34	Week 35	Week 36
Comprehension	Drawing conclusions	Making predictions	Visualization	Finding the main idea	Visualization	Compare and contrast	Sequencing events	Compare and contrast	Making inferences
Spelling	Irregular past tense verbs	Split digraphs	Digraphs: ea, ee	Endings: ar, er, or	Digraphs: ai, a–e	Word building	Suffixes: er, est	Tricky words	Suffixes: ment, ness
Grammar	Irregular past tense verbs	Prepositions	Adverbial phrases	Simple sentences	Punctuate simple sentences	Conjunctions	Compound sentences	Capitalizing proper nouns	Formal and informal language
Review	Spelling			Grammar			Comprehension		

Go, Go Gecko

Think marks

To help you understand what you are reading, you can use **special marks**. These help you see the parts you understand, and any new vocabulary.

- 👀 *I can see this part*
- **W** *What's this word?*
- ✓ *I understand this part*

Read the passage.

Use 👀 for parts of the story you can see.

Use a **W** for words you didn't know the meaning of.

Place a ✓ next to the part of the story you understand.

The Chalk Box

The chalk box moves! The class gasps. Just a tiny gasp each, but together it makes the sound of a gust of wind.

Mr. Mooney turns around. We're sitting quietly, so there's nothing he can say.

Mr. Mooney turns back to the board. We go back to staring at the chalk box.

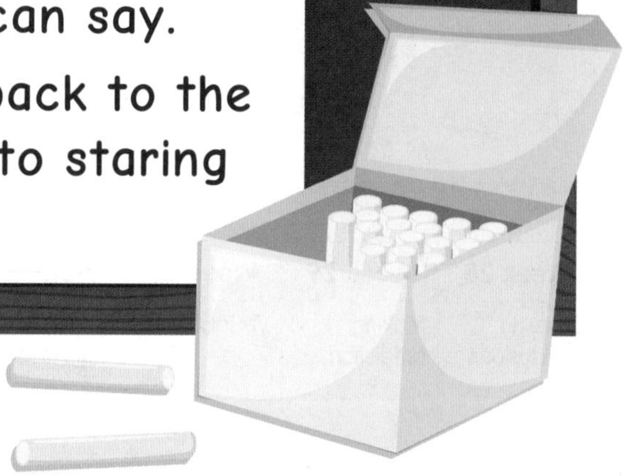

Circle the correct answer.

1. **What** are the children watching?
   - a Mr. Mooney
   - b chalk box
   - c gust of wind
   - d board
2. **Who** is sitting quietly?
   - a the class
   - b the gecko
   - c Mr. Mooney
   - d the principal
3. **What** is moving?
   - a the chalk box
   - b the wind
   - c the board
   - d the class
4. **What** is a *gasp*?
   - a the sound of the wind
   - b a quick intake of breath
5. Which word could replace *turns* in this story?
   - a spins
   - b pushes
   - c circles
   - d shows

Go, Go Gecko

Read the passage.

Use Think Marks to help you understand the passage.

Box **what** Mr. Mooney's face looks like.

Underline **where** the gecko climbs.

A Gecko on the Teacher!

The gecko jumps onto Mr. Mooney's hand. It runs up his arm. It leaps onto his head and waves at us.

Mr. Mooney's eyes roll up and his mouth is the shape of an O.

His arms freeze halfway to his head, as if he's too afraid to move.

1. **What** is the gecko doing?

____

____

2. **How** does Mr. Mooney feel?

____

____

3. Write about a time when you were really surprised by something.

____

____

Week 1 Day 3 Spelling

Verb endings: s, es

The **suffix s** can be added to a verb to make it agree with its subject; e.g., Trees grow. A tree grow**s**. If the verb ends in s, sh, ch, x, or z, add **es**; e.g., The bees buzz. The bee buzz**es**.

1 Copy each list word.

chops ______	melts ______	dances ______
bites ______	hammers ______	listens ______
bumps ______	crosses ______	blesses ______
fixes ______	breaks ______	munches ______
grows ______	buys ______	pushes ______
chases ______	behaves ______	coaches ______
hurts ______	covers ______	

2 Underline the spelling mistake. Write the word correctly.

a She dancess to the music. ______

b He listenes to the radio. ______

c Mario breakes the stick in half. ______

d Dad buyes food at the shops. ______

3 Unscramble the letters to make a list word.

a ssescro ______ b versco ______

c ltsme ______ d havesbe ______

e chescoa ______ f ersmham ______

4 Write the name for each.

a 

m ______

b 

d ______

c 

b ______

L.2.2 Demonstrate command of the conventions of standard English capitalization, punctuation, and spelling when writing.

Verb endings: s, es

1 Turn each word into a list word.

chop	chops
break	
push	

bite	
grow	

Challenge words

2 Copy each challenge word.

polishes ____________ finishes ____________

vanishes ____________ switches ____________

touches ____________ attaches ____________

launches ____________ measures ____________

teaches ____________ guesses ____________

3 Use as many challenge words as possible to make a silly story.

____

____

____

4 Color the correct word to complete each sentence.

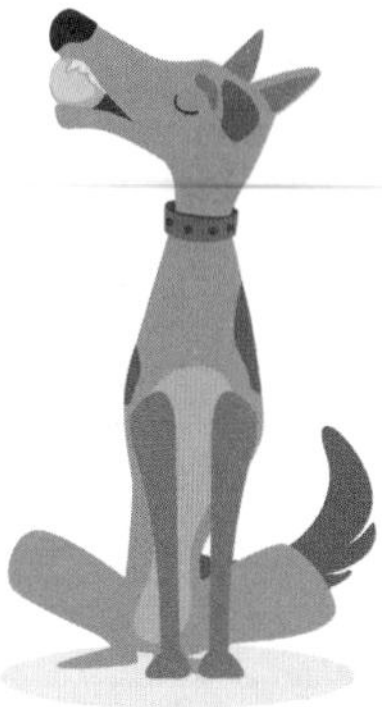

a Dad always finishes finish his dinner before me.

b The carpenter measure measures each piece of wood.

c The rain vanishes vanish when the sun comes out.

d Jack teach teaches his dog how to fetch.

e Before going to bed, Dad switches switch off all the lights.

L.2.2 Demonstrate command of the conventions of standard English capitalization, punctuation, and spelling when writing.

Common nouns

A **noun** names a person, place, animal, or thing. A **common noun** names a general person, place, animal, or thing; e.g., girl, park, dog, cup.

1 Draw lines to match the noun to the picture.

a 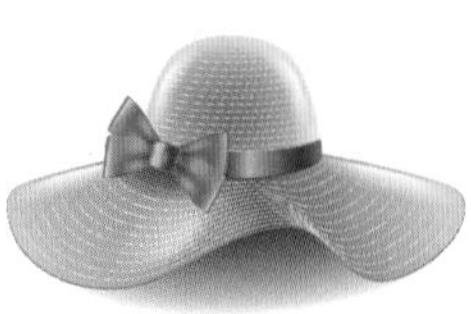

b 

c 

d 

e 

cyclist   sun   house   hat   pig

2 Draw lines to match the columns.

a bus	place
b baby	animal
c monkey	thing
d museum	person

3 Label the pictures.

a 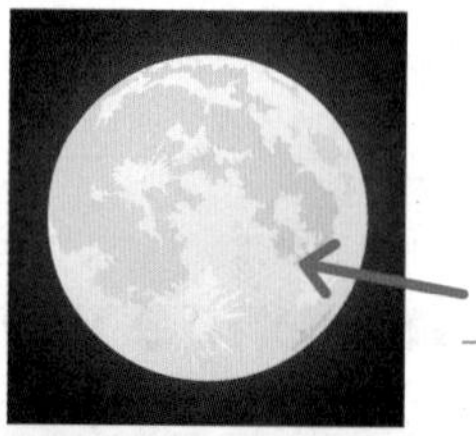 ______________________

b 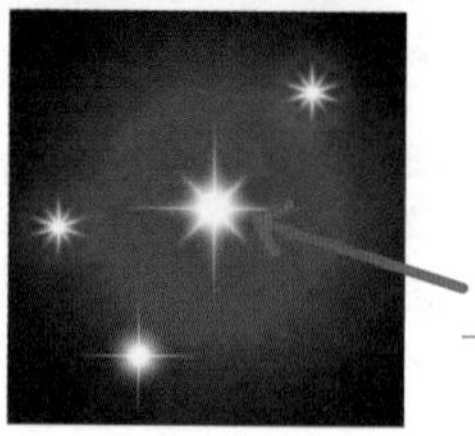 ______________________

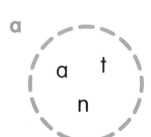

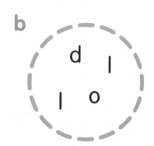

4 Use the letters in the circle to make a noun.

a a t n ______________________

b d l l o ______________________

L.2.1 Demonstrate command of the conventions of standard English grammar and usage when writing or speaking.

Tim's Money Tree

Finding facts and information

To find facts and information in a text, ask the questions **Who? What? Where?** or **When?** The answers can be clearly seen in the text.

Read the passage.

A Good Idea

"Haven't you ever seen a money tree?" asked Mandy.

Tim shook his head. "How do people get a money tree?"

"Easy!" Mandy laughed. "They plant a coin in a pot full of dirt. Then they water it."

"When the coin grows into a tree, flowers grow on it. The flowers turn into money," she told him.

Box **what** the flowers grow into.

Circle **who** is asking about a tree.

Underline **what** type of tree Tim is asking about.

Color **where** to plant the coin.

Circle the correct answer.

1. **Who** is explaining the money tree?

   a Mandy b Tim c Mom d Sam

2. **What** is the first step to grow a money tree?

   a Prune the tree. b Plant a coin.
   c Water the plant. d Pick the flowers.

3. **Where** do you grow a money tree?

   a in the forest b next to a bank
   c in a pot d by a lake

Tim's Money Tree

Read the passage.

Circle who was playing tricks.

Box what Mandy needed to do.

Underline what Mandy wanted to buy.

Trouble!

Mom didn't like Mandy playing tricks on Tim.

"There's only one thing to do," Mom said. "Take the coins out of your piggybank and stick them on Tim's tree."

"But I was saving up to buy a book!" Mandy told her.

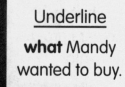

1. **Who** was playing tricks? ______________________________

2. **What** does Mom want Mandy to do? ______________________________

____

3. **Why** must Mandy do this? ______________________________

____

4. **What** had Mandy been saving for? ______________________________

RL.2.1 Ask and answer such questions as who, what, where, when, why, and how to demonstrate understanding of key details in a text.

Week 2 Day 3 Spelling

Digraphs: ar, or

Two letters that make a single sound are called a **digraph**. The letters **ar** can make the **single sound ar**; e.g., st**ar**, or the **single sound or**; e.g., w**ar**.

The letters **or** can make the **single sound or**; e.g., b**or**n, or the **single sound er**; e.g., w**or**m.

1 Copy each list word.

arm ______	ward ______	wart ______
war ______	warn ______	warp ______
car ______	born ______	apart ______
worm ______	storm ______	sport ______
work ______	short ______	spark ______
warm ______	shark ______	stork ______
word ______	snort ______	

2 Label the pictures using list words.

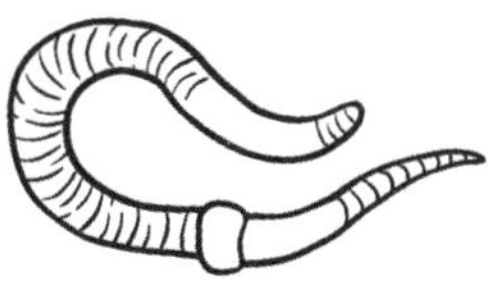

w ______

s ______

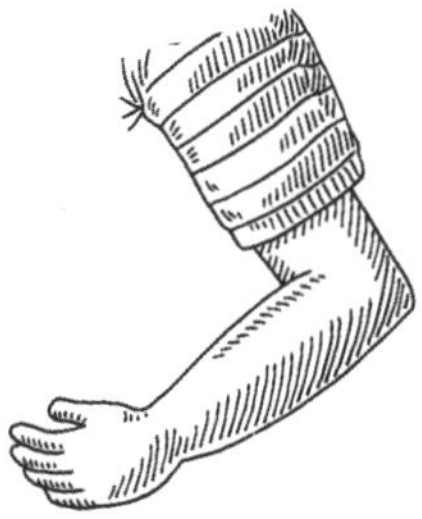

a ______

s ______

3 Sort the list words.

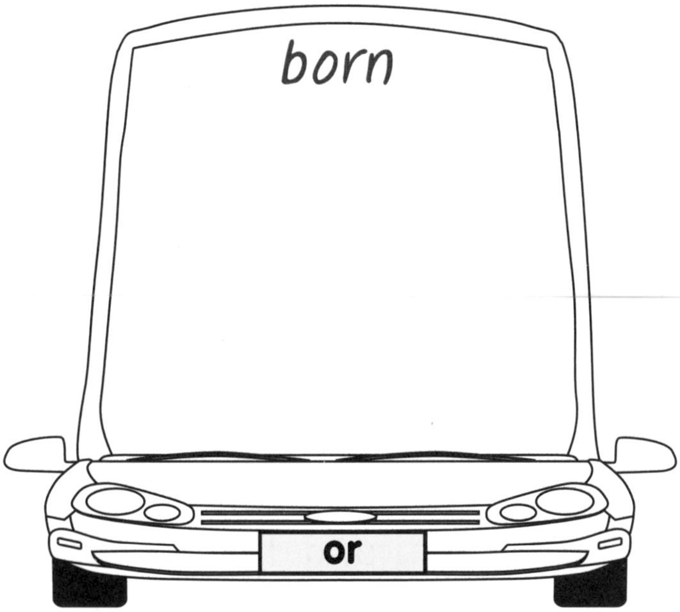

Digraphs: ar, or

1 Complete each sentence with a list word.

a In summer the weather is very ______________.

b Baseball is my favorite ______________.

c Mom drove us to practice in her new ______________.

d A ______________ has a large fin and lives in the ocean.

e The toad had a huge ______________ on his nose.

Challenge words

2 Copy each challenge word.

morning	______________	worth	______________
corner	______________	wharf	______________
normal	______________	toward	______________
world	______________	worship	______________
worse	______________	remark	______________

3 Make six words using letters from toward.

______________ ______________ ______________

______________ ______________ ______________

4 Color the correct word to complete each sentence.

a I have breakfast in the [morning] [moorning].

b We saw boats dock at the [wherf] [wharf].

c We bought ice cream at the [corner] [cerner] shop.

d They ran [toward] [toword] the finish line.

L.2.2 Demonstrate command of the conventions of standard English capitalization, punctuation, and spelling when writing.

Collective nouns

A **collective noun** names a **group** of people, animals, or things; e.g., a **crowd** of people, a **herd** of cattle.

1 Complete each phrase with a noun from the box.

a a ________________ of sheep

b a ________________ of lions

c a ________________ of shoes

d a ________________ of whales

e a ________________ of bees

f a ________________ of ships

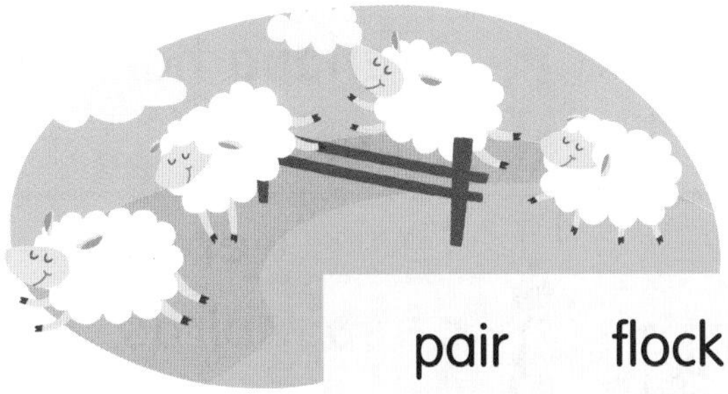

pair flock
fleet pride
swarm pod

2 Draw lines to match the collective nouns to the pictures.

a 

b 

c 

school band litter

3 Write the words next to each phrase under the correct headings.

	Collective noun		Common noun
a	a ________________	of	________________
b	a ________________	of	________________
c	a ________________	of	________________

gang thieves
library books
flowers bunch

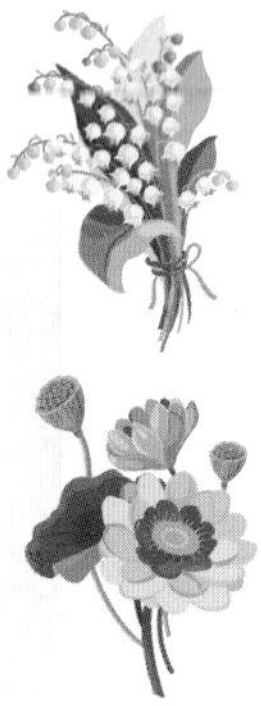

L.2.1.A Use collective nouns.

Songbird

Making inferences

To make inferences while reading, look for **clues** in the text.

The clues help you find the answers that are hiding in the text.

Read the text.

Circle **who** was in the park.

Box **what** the birds did at the park.

Underline **where** the cages hung.

Color **what** the grandpas did at the park.

Happy Birds

Lots of cages hung in the trees. Grandpa hung Yan's cage with the others.

There were lots of grandpas and lots of songbirds. All the birds whistled.

The air was full of whistles. Grandpa sat on a bench and whistled too.

Yan liked to sing with the other birds. Grandpa liked to whistle with the other grandpas.

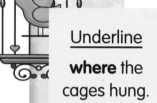

Circle the correct answer.

1. **How** did the birds feel about going to the park?

   a scared b angry c confused d happy

2. Which **clues** tell you this?

   a Lots of cages hung in the trees.
   b Yan liked to sing with the other birds.
   c All the birds whistled.
   d Grandpa hung Yan's cage.

3. What **inference** can we make about the birds?

   a Birds sing when they are happy.
   b Birds like being in cages at the park.
   c Birds are good for grandpas.
   d Birds shouldn't be kept in cages.

RL.2.3 Describe how characters in a story respond to major events and challenges.

Songbird

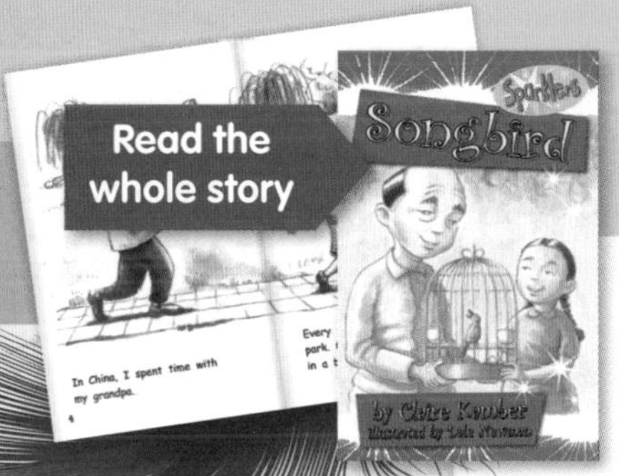

Read the letter.

Circle **the colors** of the birds.

Box **how** the birds sing.

Underline **what** Ling wants.

Color **what** Ling misses.

Dear Grandpa,

The birds in Australia have bright feathers. Some are gray and pink. Others are white and wear yellow hats. They all sing very loudly.

I wish you could hear the birds, Grandpa. They are happy birds. I am sure Yan would be happy in Australia. You would be happy too.

I miss going to the park with you, Grandpa.

Love, Ling

1. **How** do we know Ling likes Australian birds?

2. Does Ling want her Grandpa to come to Australia? How do we know?

Endings: y, ey

The **ee sound** at the end of a word is usually spelled as **y**; e.g., pupp**y**, stor**y**. Sometimes it is spelled **ey**; e.g., monk**ey**, hon**ey**.

1 Copy each list word.

any		worry		empty	
many		sixty		trolley	
ugly		honey		ninety	
key		busy		hockey	
money		twenty		seventy	
donkey		turkey		pretty	
valley		fairy			

2 Unscramble the letters to make a list word.

a ckhoey ____________

b onmey ____________

c nenity ____________

d typret ____________

e neyho ____________

f rutkey ____________

3 Write the name for each.

a

t ____________

b
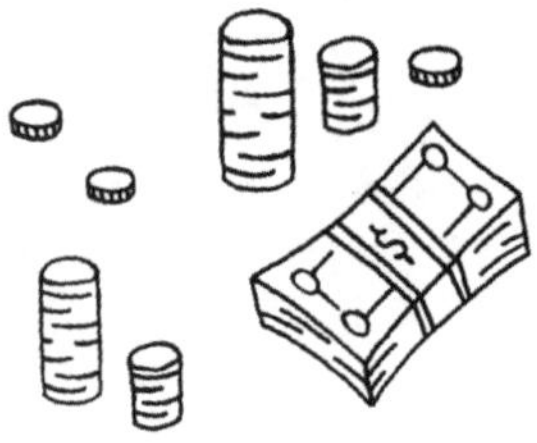
m ____________

c

d ____________

d

k ____________

4 Underline the spelling mistake. Write the word correctly.

a She put her mony in her purse. ____________

b Ten less than one hundred is ninty. ____________

c I hope to one day play hocky for the Nashville Predators. ____________

L.2.2 Demonstrate command of the conventions of standard English capitalization, punctuation, and spelling when writing.

Endings: y, ey

1 Put these list words into alphabetical order.

fairy any ugly donkey empty

_______ _______ _______ _______ _______

Challenge words

2 Copy each challenge word.

parsley ________	library ________
family ________	chimney ________
country ________	every ________
jersey ________	January ________
journey ________	February ________

3 Answer the question with a challenge word.

a What does smoke come out of? ________

b What is the first month of the year? ________

c Where can you find lots of books? ________

d What grows in your garden? ________

e Who do you live with? ________

4 Read the clue and complete each sentence using a challenge word.

a I am a shirt you wear while playing sport. I am a ________.

b I come right after January. I am ________.

c I allow you to read and borrow books. I am a ________.

d I am the land outside big cities. I am the ________.

Proper nouns

A **proper noun** names a particular person, place, animal, thing, day, or month. Proper nouns always start with a **capital letter**; e.g., **A**lex, **S**mith, **W**ednesday, **O**ctober.

1 Complete each sentence with a proper noun.

a My name is ______________________.

b I was born in the month of ______________________.

c The last month of the year is ______________________.

d My best friend's name is ______________________.

e President Lincoln's first name was ______________________.

2 Write the names of the days of the week.

______________________ ______________________

______________________ ______________________

______________________ ______________________

____

3 In each sentence, underline the word that needs a capital letter. Write it correctly in the space.

a I let ben ride my bicycle. ______________________

b I decided to call my dog bailey. ______________________

c We are going on vacation in august. ______________________

d Our neighbors' surname is brown. ______________________

e Aunt hilda is coming to visit us. ______________________

L.2.1 Demonstrate command of the conventions of standard English grammar and usage when writing or speaking.

Miss Feline's Unusual Pets

Finding the main idea

The main idea of a text is its key point. It sums up what the text is about.

Details in the text can help you find the main idea.

Read the passage.

Circle the **animals**.

Box Stella's **dialogue**.

More Unusual Pets

A goose flew in through the window. She landed with a thump. She grumbled as she got up off the floor.

Then a hyena came to the door. He had the hiccups. He saw the goose and laughed.

They began to argue. It went on and on until Stella yelled, "Stop!"

The room was silent. The crocodile stood very still.

Underline **how** the goose came through the window.

Color **what** made Stella yell.

Circle the correct answer/s.

1. What is the **main idea** of the text?

   a Stella has ordinary pets.
   b Stella doesn't want the animals to fight.
   c Stella is excited.
   d Stella is angry with the goose.

2. Which sentence **supports** the **main idea**?

   a A goose flew in through the window. She landed with a thump.
   b Then a hyena came to the door. He had the hiccups.
   c They began to argue. It went on and on until Stella yelled, "Stop!"
   d The room was silent. The crocodile stood very still.

Miss Feline's Unusual Pets

Read the passage.

Circle the rabbit's **dialogue**.

Box **how** the lion **felt**.

Underline the lion's **dialogue**.

Color the **clue** that the lion was tasting the rabbit.

Rabbit Chase

"Help! Help!" yelled the rabbit. "The lion is trying to eat me!"

"I am not," said the lion. He sounded hurt. "I was trying to whisper in your ear. But one of your whiskers tickled my nose. I just slipped.

"Then your foot was in my mouth. I don't know how that happened. Mmmmmm, yummy."

1. Fill in the missing words.

   The main idea of the text is that the ________________

   tried to eat the ________________.

2. Which **two details** helped you find the **main idea**?

   a The rabbit says, ________________

   ____

   b The lion says, ________________

   ____

RL.2.2 Recount stories, including fables and folktales from diverse cultures, and determine their central message, lesson, or moral.

scr, spr, str

In words that start with the letters **scr**, **spr**, and **str**, you can hear all three letters in the sound; e.g., **scr**eam, **spr**ang, **str**ung.

1 Copy each list word.

street	sprint	stream
spray	scrape	string
scrub	strip	scream
strong	strain	streak
stroke	struck	stride
strap	stripe	spring
strike	screen	

2 Sort the list words.

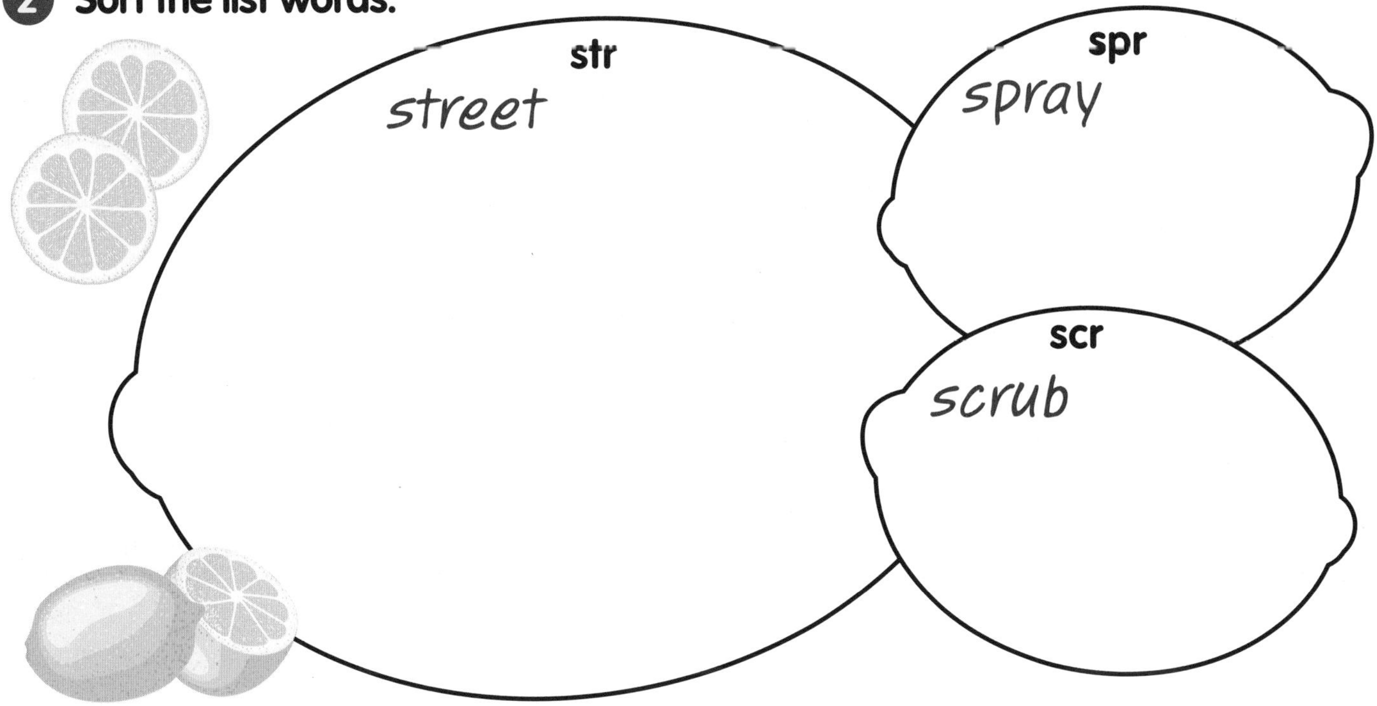

3 Match these list words to their word shapes.

street strap stroke

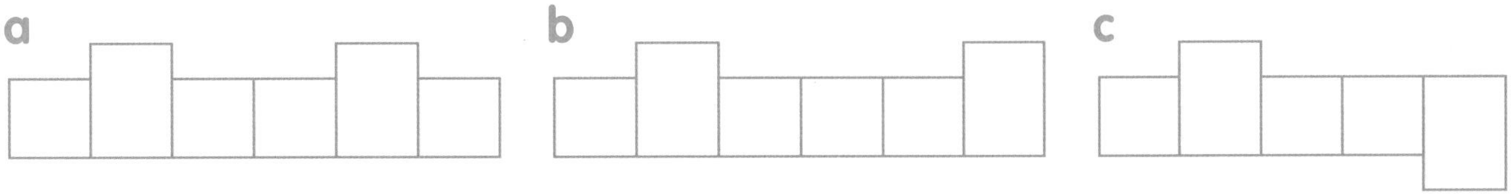

scr, spr, str

1 Underline the spelling mistake. Write it correctly.

a The kitten played with the ball of streng. ______

b I came second in the sprent. ______

c My sister was blocking the television scren. ______

d Our dog has a white strype on his head. ______

e On hot days we swim in the cool streem. ______

Challenge words

2 Copy each challenge word.

strange	______	strength	______
stroll	______	struggle	______
scribble	______	screech	______
scramble	______	strict	______
sprinkle	______	sprout	______

3 Color the correct word to complete each sentence.

a Our new coach is very [stroll] [strict].

b We took a [stroll] [strange] through the gardens.

c I saw the car [screech] [scribble] to a stop.

d I used my umbrella when it started to [sprinkle] [sprout].

4 Use as many challenge words as possible to make a silly story.

______

______

______

 L.2.2 Demonstrate command of the conventions of standard English capitalization, punctuation, and spelling when writing.

Personal pronouns

A **pronoun** stands in place of a **noun**. Using pronouns saves us repeating nouns all the time; e.g., Jacob said **Jacob** would help **Mia**. Jacob said **he** would help **her**.

1 Circle the pronoun that correctly completes each sentence.

a (Me, I) have a dog and a cat.

b (They, Them) are playing in the garden.

c I gave (he, him) an art set for his birthday.

d Why is (she, her) standing in the rain?

e Grandma and Grandpa are coming to visit (us, we).

2 Complete each sentence with a personal pronoun from the box.

a Riley helped ____________ with my model airplane.

b ____________ are eating their lunch.

c Have ____________ made your bed?

d She dropped ____________ on the floor.

e ____________ can't find her saxophone.

me you
she it they

3 Draw lines to match the pronoun to the picture.

a

b

c

d

him it them her

The Ant and the Dove

Finding the main idea

The main idea of a text is its key point. It sums up what the text is about.

Details in the text can help you find the main idea.

Read the passage.

Circle **the adjective** that describes the water.

Box **what** the dove did with the leaf.

Underline **what** the water did to the ant.

A thirsty ant came to the edge of a river to get a drink. The fast-moving water splashed the ant and knocked it into the river. The ant was in trouble! It tried to swim, but it was drowning.

A dove sitting in a tree picked a leaf and dropped it in the river, near the ant. The ant climbed onto the leaf and floated to safety on the bank of the river.

Circle the correct answer/s.

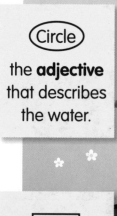

1. Which **best** describes the main idea of the text?

   a A dove saved an ant.
   b An ant fell in the water.
   c An ant was thirsty.
   d A dove was flying by the river.

2. Which **two details support** the **main idea**?

   a The water was moving quickly.
   b Ants aren't good swimmers.
   c A dove dropped a leaf in the river.
   d The leaf floated to safety.

3. Which **best** describes the dove's actions?

   a excited
   b kind
   c worried
   d angry

RL.2.2 Recount stories, including fables and folktales from diverse cultures, and determine their central message, lesson, or moral.

The Ant and the Dove

Read the passage.

(Circle) **what** the hunter did when he saw the dove.

[Box] **why** the dove flew away.

Underline **what** the ant did to the hunter.

A little while later, a hunter came to the edge of the river. He saw the dove sitting in the tree and quickly drew his bow and aimed at the resting bird. The ant saw what was about to happen. It ran over to the hunter and bit his toe as hard as it could. The hunter cried out and dropped his bow. The dove was startled and flew away to safety.

1. Fill in the missing words.

   This text is about how the ____________________

   saved the ____________________.

2. Which **two details** helped you find the **main idea**?

   a The ant ____________________

   ____

   b The hunter ____________________

   ____

Week 5 Day 3 **Spelling**

Digraph: qu

Two letters that make a single sound are called a **digraph**. The letters **qu** make the **single sound kw**; e.g., **qu**iz, **qu**ote, **qu**ick.

1 Copy each list word.

queen ______	quill ______	quake ______
quiz ______	quilt ______	squint ______
quack ______	quote ______	query ______
quit ______	equal ______	quiver ______
quite ______	equip ______	squeak ______
quest ______	quail ______	squirrel ______
quiet ______	quaint ______	

2 Write a rhyming word from the list.

a shake, make, ______

b scene, bean, ______

c shiver, liver, ______

d wrote, float, ______

e chest, best, ______

f whizz, fizz, ______

3 Which list word answers the riddle?

a I live in a castle and sit on a throne. ______

b A mouse can make this sound. ______

c I like acorns and have a big furry tail. ______

d You put me on your bed when it gets cold. ______

e A duck makes this sound. ______

4 Write the name for each.

a 

q ______

b 

q ______

c 

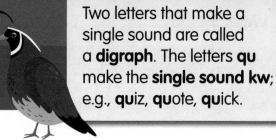

s ______

L.2.2 Demonstrate command of the conventions of standard English capitalization, punctuation, and spelling when writing.

Digraph: qu

1 Complete the list words.

a __qua__ b ____it c eq__i__

d q__es__ e qu__t__ f qu__i__t

Challenge words

2 Copy each challenge word.

queasy	________	sequin	________
squelch	________	require	________
qualify	________	quench	________
quarrel	________	question	________
frequent	________	squabble	________

3 Color the correct word to complete each sentence.

a I felt [queasy] [qweasy] after eating too much candy.

b I drank water to [qwench] [quench] my thirst.

c I raised my hand to ask her a [question] [qwestion].

d I felt the snail [sqwelch] [squelch] under my shoe.

4 Rearrange the chunks to make a list word.

a qu fre ent ________

b ab squ ble ________

c es on ti qu ________

d en ch qu ________

e el ch squ ________

Articles and nouns

Articles are the words **a**, **an**, and **the**. You use them with nouns; e.g., **a** cow, **an** egg, **the** book. Use **a** in front of a word that starts with a consonant sound; e.g., **a** taco. Use **an** in front of a word that starts with a vowel sound; e.g., **an** apple.

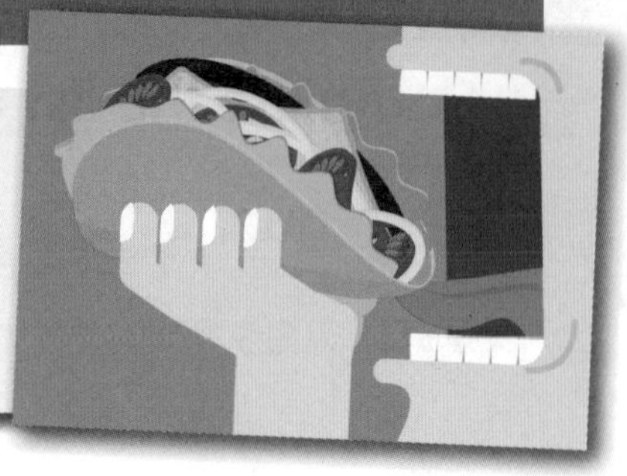

1 Fill in *a* or *an*.

a There is ______ fly in my soup.

b The story is about ______ astronaut.

c ______ ant is ______ insect.

d She drew ______ picture of ______ clown.

e He read ______ book about ______ elephant.

2 Complete the story by filling in *a, an,* or *the*.

Once upon a __________ time there was b __________ girl called Lily. She went to c __________ shops to buy d __________ ice cream. On e __________ way she met f __________ armadillo. She got g __________ shock!

3 Complete the labels with *a* or *an*.

a

______ alligator

b

______ zebra

c

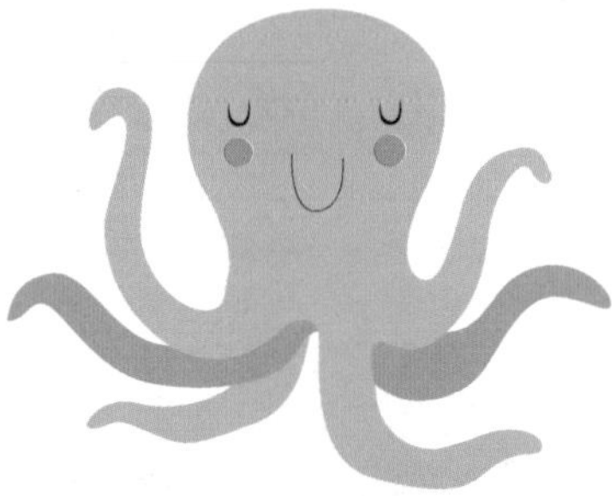

______ octopus

L.2.1 Demonstrate command of the conventions of standard English grammar and usage when writing or speaking.

Summer

Finding facts and information

To find facts and information in a text, ask the questions **Who? What? Where?** or **When?** The answers can be clearly seen in the text.

Read the passage.

Circle what flowers make in summer.

Box what covers trees in summer.

Plants in Summer

Plants grow quickly in summer.

Many plants flower in summer. Flowers make seeds. Some flowers, like apple blossoms, become fruit. Fruit grows and ripens in the summer.

In summer, trees are covered in green leaves. The leaves make food for the tree. The trunk grows thicker.

Color what happens to fruit in summer.

Underline what happens to tree trunks in summer.

Circle the correct answer.

1. **When** do apple blossoms become fruit?

   a summer b spring c winter d fall

2. **What** do the leaves of a tree do in summer?

   a attract insects b make food for the tree
   c make roots d protect the trunk

3. **What** ripens in summer?

   a leaves b trees c fruit d flowers

Summer

Read the passage.

Circle summer **foods**.

Underline summer **activities**.

Summer Food

We eat more fresh food in summer.

Salads are made from fresh summer vegetables. Families enjoy the outdoors by having picnics and barbecues.

Many fruits, such as berries, melons, and peaches, are ripe in the summer. Fruit salad is good for you and tastes good too.

1. **What** do we eat more of in summer? ____________________

2. **What** ingredients go into a salad? ____________________

3. **Where** do families enjoy barbecues? ____________________

4. **What** are some summer fruits? ____________________

5. **What** can be made with summer fruits? ____________________

RI.2.1 Ask and answer such questions as who, what, where, when, why, and how to demonstrate understanding of key details in a text.

Week 6 Day 3 Spelling

Suffixes: ing, ed

Adding the **suffix ing** to a verb shows that something is still happening; e.g., wash**ing**. When the verb ends in e, drop the e before adding ing; e.g., ride → rid**ing**.

Adding **ed** to a verb shows that something has already happened; e.g., ask**ed**. When the verb ends in e, just add **d**; e.g., hop**ed**.

1 Copy each list word.

saving ______

closed	______	agreed	______	shaped	______
hiking	______	giving	______	writing	______
freed	______	sharing	______	gazing	______
posing	______	changed	______	solved	______
used	______	phoned	______	exploded	______
raced	______	wasting	______		
chased	______	teased	______		

2 Sort the list words.

ing

saving

ed

closed

3 Unscramble the letters to make a list word.

a sedclo ______

b hsaring ______

c kihing ______

d singpo ______

e angedch ______

f eedfr ______

Suffixes: ing, ed

1 Underline the spelling mistake. Write the word correctly.

a The dog chaased the cat around the garden. ______

b The balloon explooded in her face. ______

c He finally sollved the puzzle. ______

d I agred to help set up the bake sale. ______

Challenge words

2 Copy each challenge word.

arriving ______	created ______
argued ______	freezing ______
chuckling ______	survived ______
caused ______	completed ______
shining ______	compared ______

3 Color the correct word to complete each sentence.

a The weather was [freezing] [freezeing] outside.

b My brother and I [createed] [created] a secret language.

c We will be [arriveing] [arriving] late because of traffic.

4 Use as many challenge words as possible to make a silly story.

______

______

______

______

L.2.2 Demonstrate command of the conventions of standard English capitalization, punctuation, and spelling when writing.

Punctuating statements

A **statement** is a **sentence** that tells something. It starts with a **capital letter** and ends with a **period**. If the personal pronoun **I** appears in the sentence, it is written with a **capital letter**; e.g., **M**y brother and **I** set the table**.**

1 Circle the words that need capital letters.

a the Moon is big and bright tonight.

b my friend and i went to the beach.

c the hen has laid some eggs.

d my puppy sleeps in a basket.

e noah and i were riding our scooters.

2 Fill in the capital letters and periods.

a there is someone at the door

b my sister can play the trumpet

c my sister and i have our own rooms

d our cousins like their new house

e emma and i have finished our chores

3 Write the sentences with the correct punctuation.

a the baby is eating his food

____

b ruby and i are sisters

____

Dry

Compare and contrast
To compare and contrast information, look for the **similarities** and **differences** between details in the text.

Read the passage.

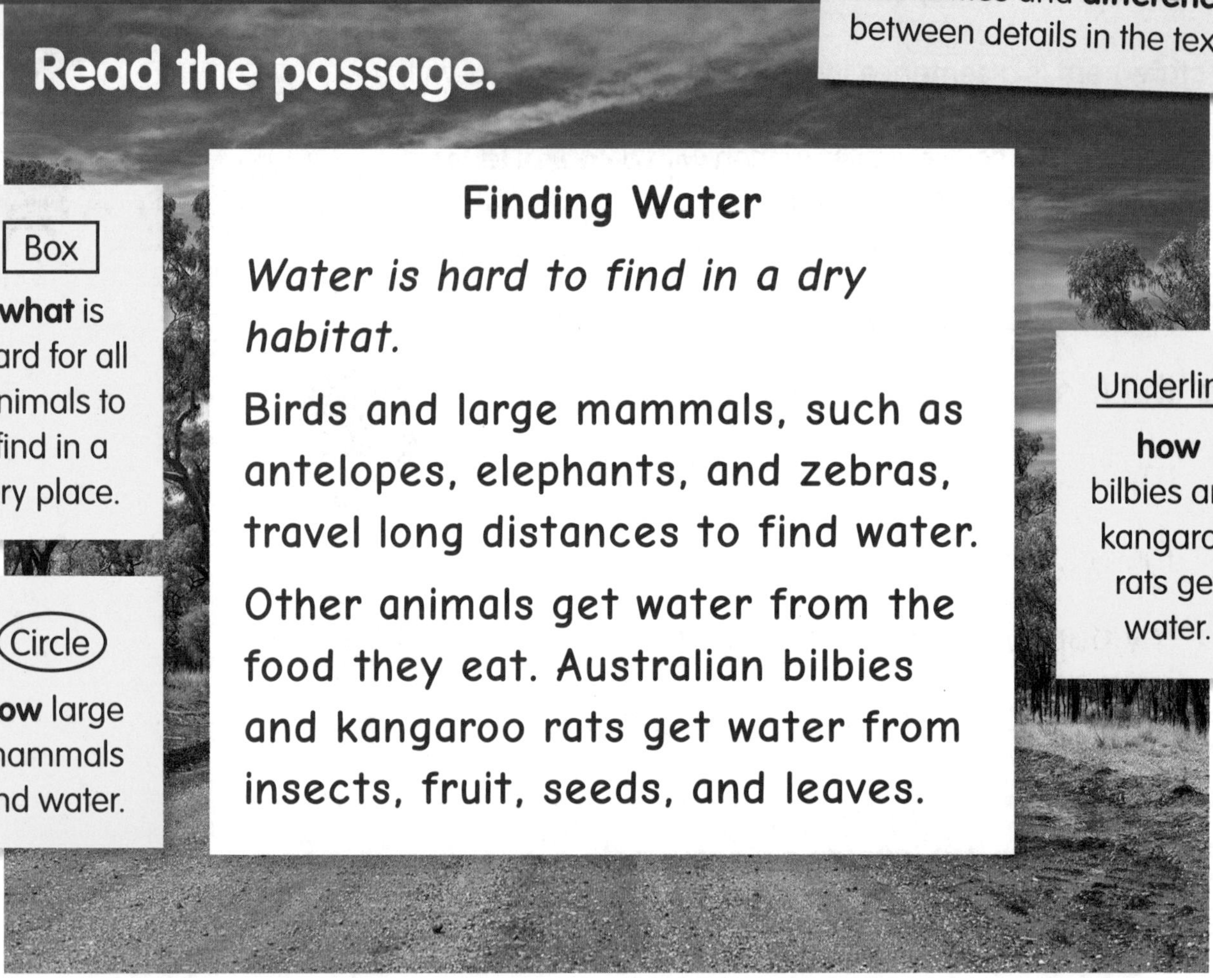

Box **what** is hard for all animals to find in a dry place.

Circle **how** large mammals find water.

Finding Water

Water is hard to find in a dry habitat.

Birds and large mammals, such as antelopes, elephants, and zebras, travel long distances to find water.

Other animals get water from the food they eat. Australian bilbies and kangaroo rats get water from insects, fruit, seeds, and leaves.

Underline **how** bilbies and kangaroo rats get water.

1 Put a [✔] next to information that is true. Put a [✘] next to information that is false.

a [ ] Antelopes and elephants are mammals.

b [ ] It is hard for all animals to find water in a dry habitat.

c [ ] Zebras drink more water than any other animal.

d [ ] Bilbies and kangaroo rats are ocean animals.

e [ ] Fruit, seeds, and leaves can give some animals water.

f [ ] Elephants are large mammals.

RI.2.1 Ask and answer such questions as who, what, where, when, why, and how to demonstrate understanding of key details in a text.

Dry

Read the passage.

Box **what** special strategies all desert animals have.

Color **how** kangaroo rats and fennec foxes stay cool.

Conserving Water

Desert animals have special water-saving strategies.

Some animals in dry habitats do not sweat to cool down. This helps the kangaroo rat and the fennec fox to conserve water.

Reptiles have thick skins. Spiders and insects have exoskeletons. These hard, outer shells reduce water loss.

Underline **how** reptiles stay cool.

1. Put a [✔] next to information that is true. Put a [✘] next to information that is false.

a [ ] The fennec fox does not sweat to help it cool down.

b [ ] All desert animals have ways to conserve water.

c [ ] Kangaroo rats have thick skins to help them save water.

d [ ] Spiders have exoskeletons to keep cool.

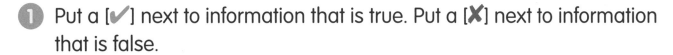

e [ ] Desert animals need to always be near water.

f [ ] An exoskeleton can help an animal reduce water loss.

Week 7 Day 3 Spelling

Prefix: un

Adding the **prefix un** to a word turns it into its **opposite**; e.g., **un**pack.

1 Copy each list word.

undo ______	unmade ______	unhappy ______
undid ______	unfair ______	undone ______
untie ______	unlike ______	unroll ______
unwise ______	unstuck ______	unable ______
unsafe ______	untrue ______	unwind ______
unfit ______	untidy ______	unload ______
unkind ______	unlock ______	

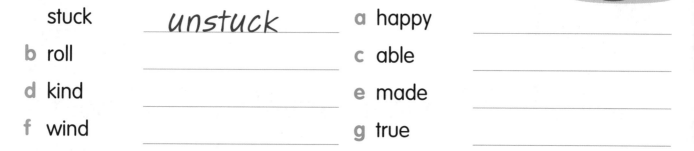

2 Write the opposites from the list.

stuck unstuck

a happy ______

b roll ______

c able ______

d kind ______

e made ______

f wind ______

g true ______

3 Write the missing letters to complete the list words.

a ___ ___ fai ___

b ___ nlik ___

c ___ ___ wis ___

d ___ ___ load

e u ___ sa ___ e

f ___ ___ fi ___

4 Build a word.

a un + true = ______

b un + fold = ______

c un + happy = ______

L.2.2 Demonstrate command of the conventions of standard English capitalization, punctuation, and spelling when writing.

Prefix: un

Challenge words

1 Copy each challenge word.

unlucky	____	unwrap	____
unknown	____	uneven	____
unbuckle	____	unhelpful	____
unusual	____	unhealthy	____
untangle	____	unfriendly	____

2 Make six words using the letters in unfriendly.

____ ____ ____

____ ____ ____

3 Color the correct word to complete each sentence.

a Some people think that black cats are [unlucky] [unluky].

b I will [unwrappe] [unwrap] my birthday presents.

c The [unfriendly] [unfrendly] boy does not have friends.

d I helped my sister [unbuckel] [unbuckle] her seatbelt.

4 Find the hidden challenge word.

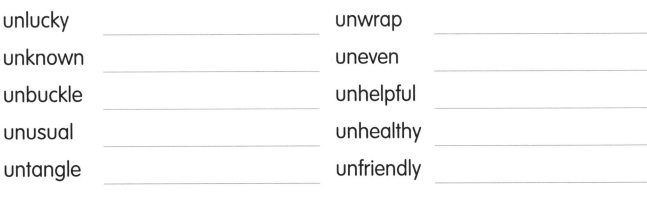

a djfunhealthysfdf ____

b dfdunhelpfuldfsdfv ____

c dfdfunusualdfdfs ____

d dfdduntangledfd ____

L.2.2 Demonstrate command of the conventions of standard English capitalization, punctuation, and spelling when writing.

Adjectives

Adjectives give information about **nouns** and **pronouns**; e.g., **three** kittens, a **disgusting** smell, **happy** children, a **kind** person.

1 Complete each sentence with an adjective from the box.

a I like to swim on ________________ days.

b My friend has a ________________ cat.

c There are ______________ eggs in the carton.

d My dad bakes ____________________ pies.

e I was __________________ when I saw the mess.

angry six
furry hot
delicious

2 Write the adjectives under the correct heading.

blue twelve brown bitter sweet
twenty purple seven spicy

How many?	What color?	What taste?
____________	____________	____________
____________	____________	____________
____________	____________	____________

3 Circle the adjectives that could describe the pizza.

delicious

crispy

square

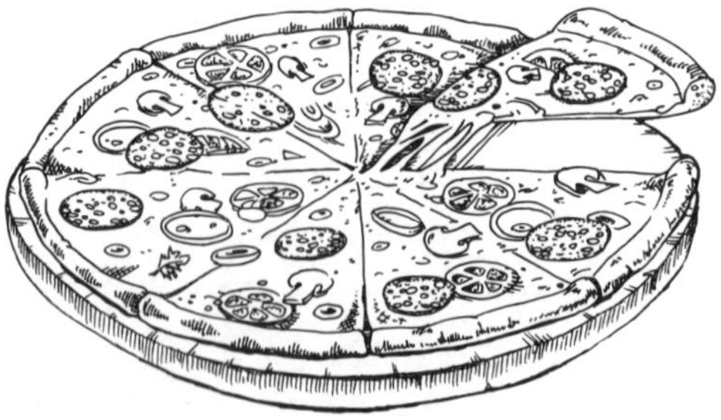

round

lazy

hot

L.2.1.E Use adjectives.

Trains

Finding the main idea

To discover what a text is about, look for the main idea or key point.

Facts and details in the text can help you find the main idea.

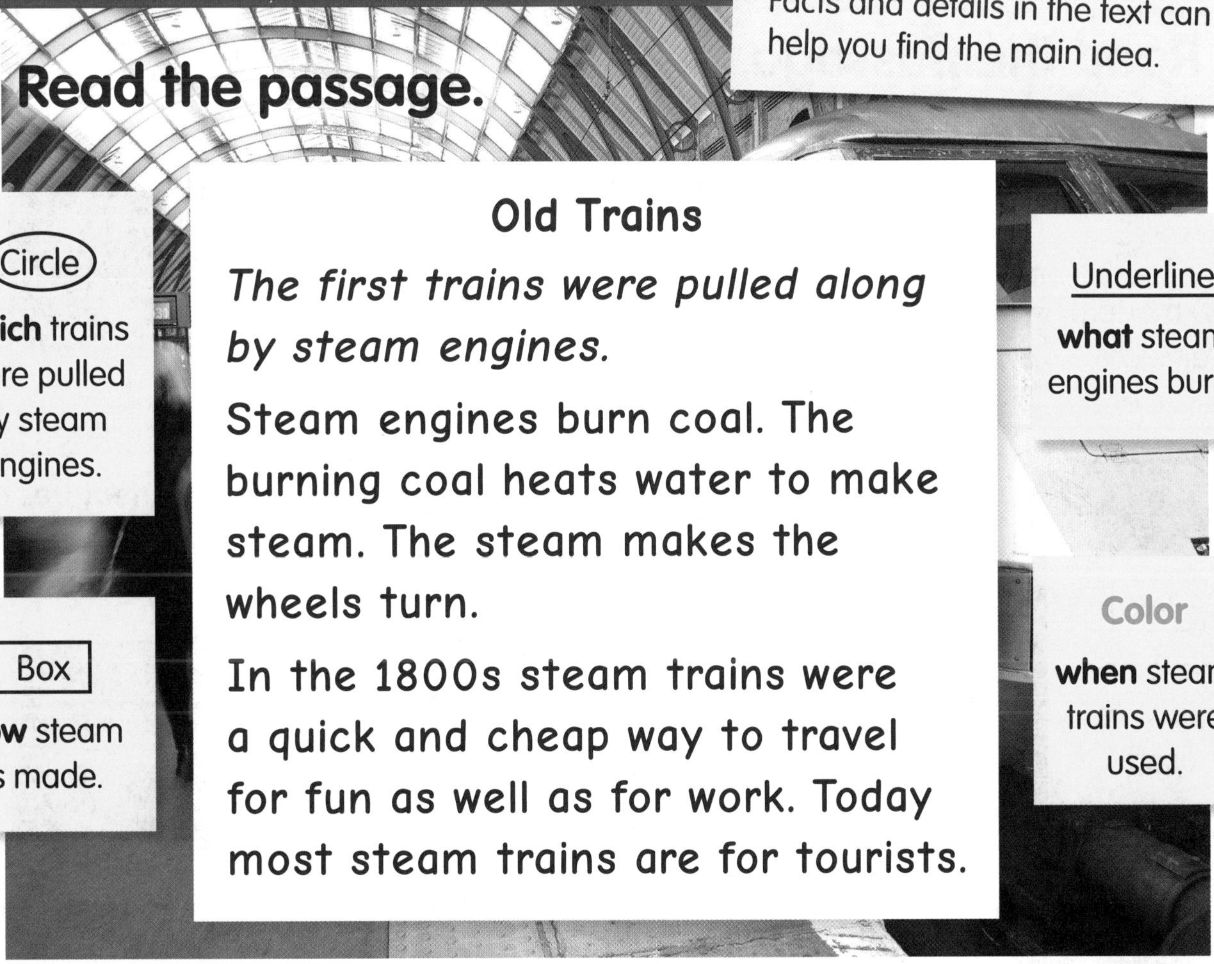

Read the passage.

Circle **which** trains were pulled by steam engines.

Box **how** steam is made.

Underline **what** steam engines burn.

Color **when** steam trains were used.

Old Trains

The first trains were pulled along by steam engines.

Steam engines burn coal. The burning coal heats water to make steam. The steam makes the wheels turn.

In the 1800s steam trains were a quick and cheap way to travel for fun as well as for work. Today most steam trains are for tourists.

Circle the correct answer/s.

1. What is the **main idea** of the text?
   - a to give facts about why train travel is fun
   - b to describe how steam trains burn coal
   - c to explain how steam trains work and were used
   - d to tell others where to ride steam trains

2. Which two sentences best **support** the **main idea**?
   - a Today most steam trains are for tourists.
   - b The first trains were pulled along by steam engines.
   - c In the 1800s steam trains were a quick and easy way to travel.
   - d The steam makes the wheels turn.

Trains

Read the passage.

Color **how** modern trains are powered.

Box **where** new trains are used.

Underline **features** of new trains.

New Trains

Today, most trains have diesel or electric engines.

The new engines are quieter and cleaner than coal-powered steam engines. Diesel trains are often used in country areas. Many electric trains run in cities.

Some electric trains can travel very fast. They are called high-speed trains. The bullet trains in Japan can travel three times faster than a car.

1. Fill in the missing words.

   This text is about different types of ______________________.

2. Give **two details** that support the **main idea**.

   a Most trains ______________________

   ____

   b New train engines ______________________

   ____

RI.2.2 Identify the main topic of a multiparagraph text as well as the focus of specific paragraphs within the text.

Digraph: oo

Two letters that make a single sound are called a **digraph**. The letters **oo** make the **single sound oo**. The digraph oo can make a **long sound**; e.g., f**oo**d, or **short sound**; e.g., c**oo**k.

1 Copy each list word.

too	hoot	goose
mood	took	proof
hook	cool	shoot
foot	tooth	loose
wood	broom	groom
room	gloom	ooze
soon	igloo	

2 Write the name for each.

a
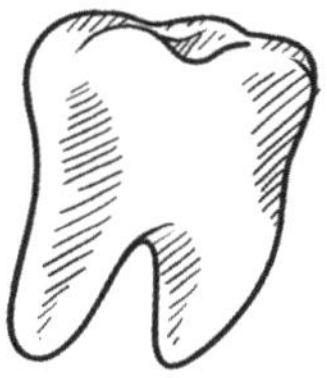
t

b
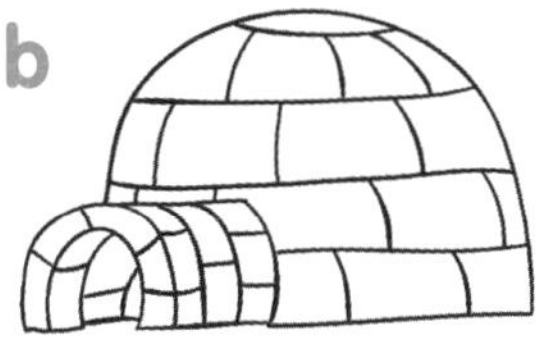
i

c
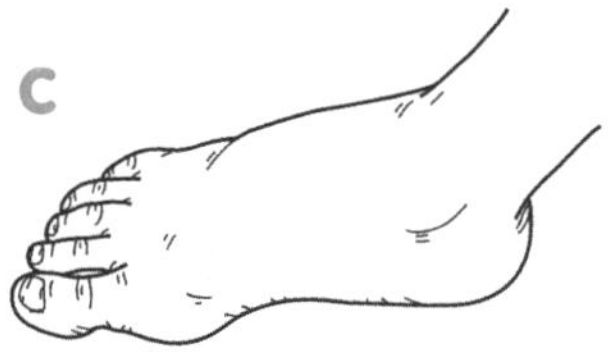
f

d

h

3 Sort the list words.

Digraph: oo

1 Fill in the missing letters.

a Mom told us to tidy our toy r__________.

b I swept up the mess with a b__________.

c He cut blocks of ice to build an i__________.

Challenge words

2 Copy each challenge word.

soothe	__________	poodle	__________
scooter	__________	boomerang	__________
rooster	__________	kangaroo	__________
school	__________	snooze	__________
goodbye	__________	cocoon	__________

3 Read the clue and find the challenge word.

a I live on a farm and sing very loudly. I am a __________.

b If you throw me, I will come back. I am a __________.

c I have two wheels and a handle bar. I am a __________.

d I am a dog with thick, curly fur. I am a __________.

e A caterpillar goes in, a butterfly comes out. I am a __________.

4 Answer the question with a challenge word.

a What do you say when you are leaving? __________

b What do you do if you're feeling tired? __________

c What has a pouch and two large feet? __________

Irregular plurals

A **plural noun** names **more than one** person, place, or thing. Most plurals are formed by adding **s** or **es** to the singular; e.g., bird**s**, peach**es**. Some nouns change in other ways when written in the plural; e.g., 1 goose → 2 geese. Others do not change at all; e.g., 1 sheep → 3 sheep.

1 Color the notes with plural nouns.

mice	mouse	women	woman
person	people	ox	oxen

2 Write the underlined word as a plural.

a The dentist filled two of my <u>tooth</u> ____________________.

b The <u>child</u> ____________________ were making a lot of noise.

c I spotted two wild <u>goose</u> ____________________ among the ducks.

d I put on socks because my <u>foot</u> ____________________ were cold.

e The <u>woman</u> ____________________ are watching the game on TV.

3 Color THREE nouns that stay the same in the plural.

animal	sheep	moose
cake	deer	horse

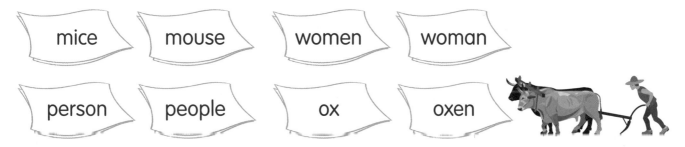

Bread

Sequencing events

To identify the sequence of events in a text, look at numbers and words that give clues to the order in which things happen.

Read the passage.

Growing Grain

Wheat, oat, rye, and rice are all grains. People eat more grain than any other food.

Farmers grow wheat in large, flat fields. They use machines called cultivators to prepare the soil for planting.

Farmers mix fertilizer with seeds to help the grain grow. They then use a seeder to drop the seeds into furrows.

1. **Order** the events to grow wheat.

☐ Use a seeder to drop seeds.

☐ Mix fertilizer with seeds.

☐ Choose your grain—wheat.

☐ Use a cultivator to prepare the soil for planting.

☐ Choose a large, flat field.

2. What would need to happen **next** for the seeds to grow? Write and draw.

RI.2.3 Describe the connection between a series of historical events, scientific ideas or concepts, or steps in technical procedures in a text.

Bread

Read the passage.

Circle **how** the wheat gets to the flour mills.

Box **how long** the grain is soaked.

Underline **what** crushes the wheat.

Refining

Trucks carry wheat to flour mills. The wheat grains are made into flour.

People inspect the wheat to make sure it is good quality.

The grain is cleaned and soaked in water for 10 to 20 hours. This separates the outer layer of bran from the soft, inner part. Rollers crush the wheat into a powder called flour.

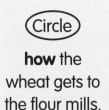

1. What happens to the wheat **before** it is soaked?

____

____

2. What happens to the wheat **after** it is soaked?

____

____

3. What does this text explain?

____

____

Soft c

The letter **c** makes a **soft s sound** when it comes **before e, i, or y**; e.g., pencil, ice.
Before the vowels a, o, u, and some consonants, it makes a **k sound**; e.g., cold, crack.

1 Copy each list word.

race	______	nice	______	price	______
ice	______	pace	______	space	______
cell	______	trace	______	grace	______
city	______	once	______	spicy	______
mice	______	slice	______		
face	______	twice	______		
icy	______	cycle	______		
lace	______	since	______		

2 Write the name for each.

a

r ______

b

f ______

c

c ______

d

m ______

3 Fill in the missing letters.

a Her dress was fringed with white l __ __ e.

b On my birthday I was given the biggest s __ __ __ e of cake.

c I enjoyed the movie so much I saw it t __ __ __ e.

d My drink was i __ __ cold.

e O __ __ e upon a time there was a princess who was just and fair.

f It was n __ __ e of him to stay and help us clean up.

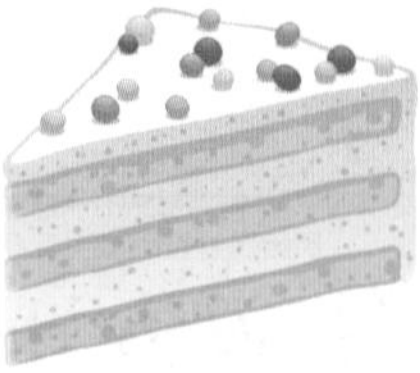

L.2.2 Demonstrate command of the conventions of standard English capitalization, punctuation, and spelling when writing.

Soft c

1 Match these list words to their word shapes.

a

b

c

d

e

cell
spicy
space
race
city

Challenge words

2 Copy each challenge word.

fleece	____________	prince	____________
peace	____________	recite	____________
juicy	____________	pencil	____________
fancy	____________	notice	____________
piece	____________	excite	____________

3 Color the correct word.

a The peach was so [juicy] [joocy] it squirted all over me.

b I used a yellow [pencel] [pencil] to color in the sun.

c The [prynce] [prince] was searching for his dragon.

d My boots have a soft [flece] [fleece] lining.

e I just wanted one more [pece] [piece] of candy.

4 Answer the question with a challenge word.

a What comes from a sheep? ____________

b What do you write with? ____________

c Who is the king's son? ____________

Commas in letters

When writing letters or notes, use a **comma** (,):
- after the person's name in the greeting; e.g., Dear Billie,
- before your own name at the close; e.g., Your friend,
Sammy

1 Fill in the missing commas.

a Dear Tess

Please come to my birthday party. It's on Saturday, October 6. It starts at 2 o'clock.

Your friend Olivia

b Dear Mr. and Mrs. Johnson

I'm sorry my dog dug holes in your garden. I won't let it happen again.

Your neighbor
Jamie Martin

2 Fill in the greetings and endings in each note.

a ____________________

Thank you for coming to my party. I really like the book you gave me. I've already finished it.

____

b ____________________

I'm so excited! Mom says you're coming to visit us next month. We'll have fun playing with my new puppy. She's so cute.

____

Spelling

Use this review to test your knowledge. It has three parts—**Spelling**, **Grammar**, and **Comprehension**. If you're unsure of an answer, go back and read the rules and generalizations in the blue boxes.

You have learned about:

- verb endings: s, es
- scr, spr, str
- prefix: un
- digraphs: ar, or
- digraph: qu
- digraph: oo
- endings: y, ey
- suffixes: ing, ed
- soft c

1 Which correctly completes the word? 1 mark

st __ __ m

a ar   b or   c ir   d er

2 Which word completes the sentence? 1 mark

Charlie __________ carrots in his garden.

a growing   b grow   c grows   d growed

3 Complete each word with *scr, spr,* or *str.* 3 marks

a __ __ __ eet   b __ __ __ ub   c __ __ __ int

4 Correct the word that is wrong in each sentence. 4 marks

a Ali made a spicey curry. __________

b I like to play hocky. __________

c I felt qeasey on the boat. __________

d We were unnhappey with the weather. __________

5 Make four words using the letters from *boomerang.* 1 mark

__________   __________

__________   __________

Your score

/10

Grammar

You have learned about:

- common nouns
- personal pronouns
- adjectives
- collective nouns
- nouns and articles
- irregular plurals
- proper nouns
- punctuating sentences
- commas in letters

1 Color the noun in each circle. 2 marks

a bird sing

b box open

2 Complete each phrase with a collective noun. 2 marks

a a ________________ of cows

b a ________________ of whales

3 In each sentence, circle the word that needs a capital letter. 2 marks

a My best friend's name is amy.

b The first month of the year is january.

4 Replace the noun in parentheses with a pronoun. 4 marks

a Annie said (Annie) ________________ didn't have enough money.

b I told Annie I would lend (Annie) ________________ two dollars.

c The children said (the children) ________________ would take the dog for a walk.

d We told the children we would help (the children) ________________.

Grammar

5 Write the correct words. 4 marks

a I added (a, an) ____________ egg to (the, an) ____________ mixture.

b I put (a, the) ____________ cupcakes on (a, an) ____________ plate.

6 Complete the sentence with two adjectives. 2 marks

My ________________________ friend has ________________________ dogs.

7 Write the plurals of the following words. 2 marks

a one foot → two ____________

b one man → two ____________

8 Fill in the missing punctuation in the following letter. 2 marks

Dear Aunt Meg

Thank you for the art set. I'm painting a picture of you and Uncle Joe. I'll send it to you when it's finished.

Your favorite niece

Jody

Your score

/ 20

Ringing Guzzler

Read the passage and then use the comprehension skills you have learned to answer the questions.

My dog eats everything. Yesterday he guzzled the sausages in Mom's shopping bag. Last week it was my homework.

This morning Mom couldn't find her cell phone. She looked on the kitchen bench, in the car, next to the bed. It was nowhere to be seen.

"Okay," said Dad, "I'll use my cell phone to call your phone."

Guzzler burped. Dad called the number. Yes! There was a faint ring. The sound was coming from somewhere near Guzzler. Oh, no! It was Guzzler! He'd guzzled Mom's phone.

Dad and I laughed, but Mom said, "We'll take Guzzler to the vet to get my phone back, but that's it! I'm going to give him away."

"No, Mom," I cried. "You can't give Guzzler away. He's mine!"

1 Why is the dog called Guzzler? 1 mark **INFERENTIAL**

a He likes sausages.
b His owner liked the name.
c He eats everything.
d He has a big belly.

2 What was in Mom's shopping bag? 1 mark **LITERAL**

a a cell phone
b sausages
c a tennis ball
d the writer's homework

Ringing Guzzler

3 Why couldn't Mom find her phone? 1 mark — LITERAL

a It was under the bed.
b It was in the car.
c It was in a kitchen drawer.
d It was inside Guzzler.

4 Which word is similar in meaning to *burped*? 1 mark — VOCABULARY

a coughed
b sneezed
c belched
d yawned

5 How did Mom know where her phone was? 1 mark — LITERAL

a She heard it ring.
b She remembered where she'd put it.
c She accidentally tripped over it.
d She saw it on the kitchen bench.

6 What did Dad and the narrator think when they found out what Guzzler had done? They thought it was ... 1 mark — INFERENTIAL

a dangerous.
b funny.
c unfair.
d silly.

7 How did Mom feel about Guzzler eating her phone? 1 mark — INFERENTIAL

a worried
b confused
c amazed
d angry

8 Who will help Mom get her phone back? 1 mark — LITERAL

a the vet
b the doctor
c Dad
d the plumber

9 What does Mom plan to do with Guzzler? 1 mark — LITERAL

a sell him
b give him away
c make him stay outside
d lock him up

10 How does the narrator feel about Mom's decision? 1 mark — INFERENTIAL

a glad
b disappointed
c upset
d scared

Your score ☐ / 10

Your Review 1 Scores

Spelling		Grammar		Comprehension		Total
☐ / 10	+	☐ / 20	+	☐ / 10	=	☐ / 40

Take Me to Your Leader

Making inferences

To make inferences while reading, look for **clues** in the text.

The clues help you find the answers that are hiding in the text.

Read the passage.

Circle the **alien's dialogue**.

Box **adjectives** that describe the **alien**.

Underline **how** Tim moves to the closet.

Color **Tim's dialogue**.

Thump! Thump! Thump!

What is that?

"Thump!"

It's coming from the closet. Tim creeps over and slides the door open. A tiny purple alien steps out and pokes Tim on the foot.

"Take me to your weader!"

Tim jumps back on the bed. The alien is only as big as a teddy bear, but he has a zap gun. The gun is pointed at Tim.

"Wha ... what?" Tim asks.

Circle the correct answer.

1. **How** does Tim feel about the alien?

   a scared b angry c confused d happy

2. Which **clue** tells you this?

   a "Thump!"
   b "Take me to your weader!"
   c What is that?
   d Tim jumps back on the bed.

3. What **inference** can we make about Tim?

   a Tim is bigger than the alien.
   b Tim has a very messy room.
   c Teddy bears are Tim's favorite toys.
   d Tim lives on a planet with aliens.

RL.2.3 Describe how characters in a story respond to major events and challenges.

Take Me to Your Leader

Read the whole story

Read the passage.

Color words that describe **Gweep's appearance.**

Box **Gweep's dialogue.**

Underline **Tim's dialogue.**

Slime Jello

"Here is some slime instead," Tim yells.

Gweep looks in the bowl. "This bad."

Tim looks at the yummy, wobbly, green jello. "It's really very nice."

Tears form in Gweep's three round eyes. "It's saying no!"

"The slime isn't saying no. It's shaking because it's scared of you."

"Is it scared?" Gweep smiles. "Of me?"

1. **Why** does Tim pretend the jello is slime?

____

____

2. We can **infer** that Gweep is happy at the end. What is the **clue**?

____

____

Plurals with y

Adding the **suffix es** to a **noun** makes it **plural**; e.g., beach**es**.

Adding the **suffix es** to a **verb** makes it **agree with its subject**; e.g., the bee buzz**es**.

If the noun or verb ends in y, change it to i before **adding es**; e.g., injury → injur**ies**, copy → cop**ies**.

1 Copy each list word.

cries	______	babies	______	ladies	______
dries	______	stories	______	entries	______
fries	______	parties	______	worries	______
spies	______	carries	______	replies	______
skies	______	cities	______	studies	______
tries	______	bodies	______	families	______
copies	______	duties	______		

2 Rewrite the word. Change y to i and add es.

a He (try) ______ to swim.

b She (spy) ______ on people.

c The (baby) ______ are crying.

d The (city) ______ are large.

e He (carry) ______ the bag.

3 Write the name for each.

a

f ______

b

b ______

c

c ______

L.2.2 Demonstrate command of the conventions of standard English capitalization, punctuation, and spelling when writing.

Plurals with y

1 Unscramble the list words.

a rrcaies ______________________ b bibaes ______________________

c iesorst ______________________ d iesarpt ______________________

e iesrrwo ______________________ f disesut ______________________

Challenge words

2 Copy each challenge word.

enemies	______________________	injuries	______________________
qualities	______________________	multiplies	______________________
properties	______________________	supplies	______________________
difficulties	______________________	factories	______________________
memories	______________________	libraries	______________________

3 Color the correct word.

a The soccer players had many [injuries] [injurys] after the game.

b He is having [difficultes] [difficulties] with his computer.

c They are closing down all the old [factories] [factorys].

d If he [multiples] [multiplies] six by two he will get twelve.

4 Write the challenge words in alphabetical order.

______________________ ______________________

______________________ ______________________

______________________ ______________________

______________________ ______________________

______________________ ______________________

Action verbs

Every sentence must have a **verb**. An **action verb** shows what action is happening; e.g., The children **run** in the park.

1 Draw lines to match the action verb to the picture.

a

b

c

d

e

eats   rides   brushes   bakes   skips

2 Complete each sentence with an action verb from the box.

a I sometimes ________________ dinner.

b She ________________ bread at the bakery.

c They ________________ their bags to the car.

d He ________________ his name on the card.

e Alex ________________ into the pool.

carry   dives   buys
cook   writes

3 Complete each sentence with an action verb.

a I ________________ the drums.

b I ________________ with a pencil.

c I ________________ at a traffic light.

d I ________________ a ball with a bat.

e I ________________ with a knife and fork.

L.2.1 Demonstrate command of the conventions of standard English grammar and usage when writing or speaking.

Mandy Made Me Do It

Visualization

Good readers imagine pictures when they read a text. This is called visualizing.

Looking for key words in the text helps you create images.

Read the passage.

Circle the **noises** Tim made.

Underline **how** Mom moved.

Beds Are Not Trampolines

Tim did a star jump. Then he fell off the bed and landed on his nose. He started to cry.

He cried louder and louder. Mom came running into the room and picked him up.

"Now what have you done?" she asked, looking at his red nose.

"Mandy made me do it," Tim sobbed.

Circle the correct answer.

1. **How** was Tim feeling?

   a scared b nervous c excited d sad

2. Which **key words** tell what Tim did?

   a running into the room b landed on his nose

3. Which word helps us **hear** how Tim was feeling?

   a landed b sobbed c nose d fell

4. Which word helps us **see** Tim's nose?

   a landed b jump c cry d red

Mandy Made Me Do It

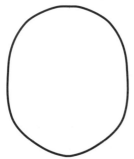

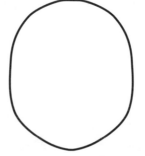

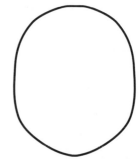

Read the passage.

Circle **what** happened to Tim's balloon.

Underline **how** Mom and Aunt Beth **felt**.

Big Trouble

Tim was in big trouble. He had climbed out the bedroom window to make a water balloon.

As he turned the water on, his balloon flew off. Water sprayed all over the yard.

Just then, Mom and Aunt Beth stepped into the garden. Both of them were sprayed with water. Boy, were they angry!

1. Imagine if you turned on water and it sprayed on you. How would you feel?

____

2. Draw Tim's **actions** from the text.

3. Re-read the story. Draw Tim, Mom, and Aunt Beth's faces at the end.

RL.2.3 Describe how characters in a story respond to major events and challenges.

Week 11 Day 3 Spelling

The j sound

The **j sound** is always spelled as **j** before a, o, and u; e.g., **j**ar, **j**ob.
The **j sound** is often spelled as **g** before e, i, and y; e.g., **g**em, **g**ym.

1 Copy each list word.

gem ______	germ ______	jewel ______
jar ______	giant ______	adjust ______
jog ______	join ______	Japan ______
jug ______	June ______	magic ______
joke ______	July ______	energy ______
jump ______	angel ______	January ______
jelly ______	giraffe ______	

2 Write the name for each.

a 
b 
c 
d 

j ______ j ______ g ______ j ______

3 Sort the list words.

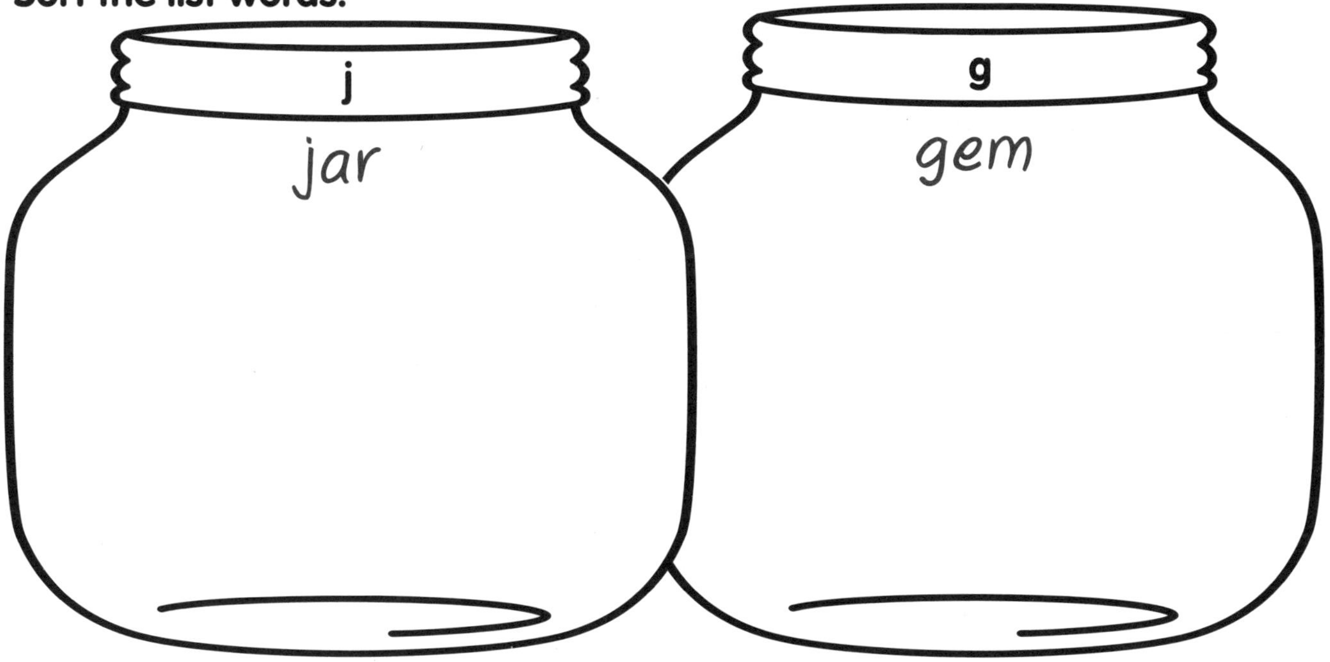

The j sound

1 Complete each sentence with a list word.

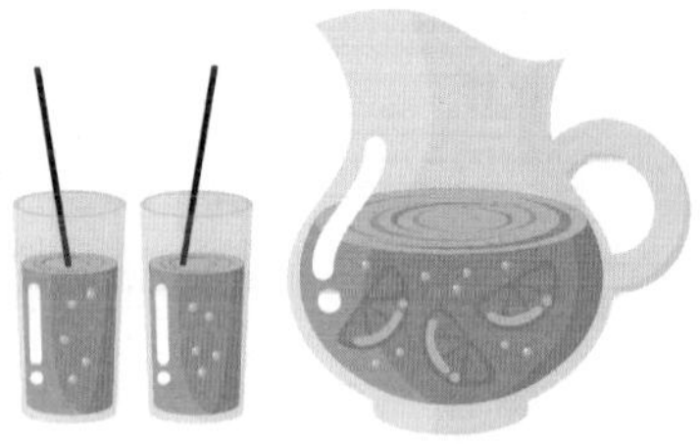

a We like to __________ on the trampoline.

b The __________ has a very long neck.

c __________ is the first month of the year.

d I poured everyone some juice from the __________.

e Everyone laughed at Mom's funny __________.

Challenge words

2 Copy each challenge word.

urgent	__________	engine	__________
agile	__________	margin	__________
jigsaw	__________	juice	__________
allergy	__________	digit	__________
fragile	__________	jacket	__________

3 Answer the question with a challenge word.

a What do you wear when it's cold? __________

b What is something that you can drink? __________

c What is under the hood of a car? __________

d What game has puzzle pieces? __________

e What is another name for a single number? __________

4 Write the challenge words in alphabetical order.

__________ __________ __________ __________ __________

__________ __________ __________ __________ __________

L.2.2 Demonstrate command of the conventions of standard English capitalization, punctuation, and spelling when writing.

Simple present and past tense

The **tense** of a verb shows **when** an action happens; e.g.,
The dogs **walk**. (Present tense → happens now.)
The dogs **walked**. (Past tense → has already happened.)

1 Sort the verbs.

walked push stopped blamed sail fill picked play

Present tense	Past tense
______	______
______	______
______	______
______	______

2 Underline the word that is wrong. Write it correctly.

a Last week Jake fix his bicycle. ______
b I enter the competition last year. ______
c I finish reading the book an hour ago. ______
d Yesterday Hayley visit her grandma. ______
e Last night I watch my favorite program. ______

3 Write these sentences in the past tense.

a I lock the door to the garage.

Yesterday ______

______

b I wash the dishes after dinner.

Last night ______

______

Saving Greedy Guts

Finding the main idea

The main idea of a text is its key point. It sums up what the text is about.

Details in the text can help you find the main idea.

Read the passage.

Circle the **verbs** about **eating**.

Gee-Gee?

When I picked him up, Greedy Guts chewed on my fingers. Then he gnawed the strap of my watch.

I put him on the floor and he untied my shoelaces. Then he tried to pull my left sock off. He loved me so much, he wanted to eat me. How could I resist him?

"Mom, please," I begged. "He's perfect."

Underline the **things** Greedy Guts tried to **eat**.

Circle the correct answer/s.

1. Find the **main idea** of the text.
   - a Greedy Guts was bought from a pet shop.
   - b Greedy Guts is perfect.
   - c Greedy Guts likes to eat everything.
   - d Greedy Guts wants to wear socks.
2. Which **two** sentences best **support** the main idea?
   - a "Mom, please," I begged. "He's perfect."
   - b We bought Greedy Guts at a pet shop.
   - c When I picked him up, Greedy Guts chewed on my fingers.
   - d Then he gnawed the strap of my watch.
   - e He loved me so much, he wanted to eat me. How could I resist him?

Saving Greedy Guts

Read the passage.

Circle **who** sent the jacket.

Color **what** the jacket looked like.

Underline **why** Mom got the jacket.

Yesterday was Mom's birthday. Aunt Minnie sent Mom a pink, fluffy jacket. Mom hates pink, and she hates fluffy.

"I must ring her to say thank you," Mom said. "Aunt Minnie is a dear to remember my birthday, even if she doesn't remember what I like," Mom said.

"Aunt Minnie is family, and you can't choose your family. Mmmm ... perhaps I could wash it and say that it shrank."

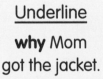

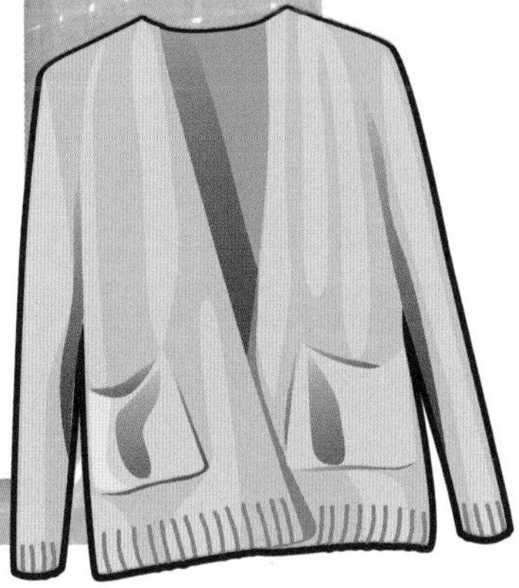

1. Fill in the missing words.

   The text is about what ____________________ thinks of

   ____________________ present.

2. Which **two details** helped you find the main idea?

   a Mom says, ____________________

   ____

   b Mom also says, ____________________

   ____

Endings: le, el, al

Most two-syllable words that end in the **l sound** have the letters **le** at the end; e.g., puddl**e**.

Some two-syllable words that end in the **l sound** have the letters **el** at the end; e.g., cam**el**.

Some two-syllable words that end in the **l sound** have the letters **al** at the end; e.g., flor**al**.

1 Copy each list word.

angel		panel		title	
oval		level		cruel	
handle		camel		parcel	
total		tunnel		dimple	
novel		puddle		towel	
noodle		signal		label	
travel		kennel			

2 Sort the list words.

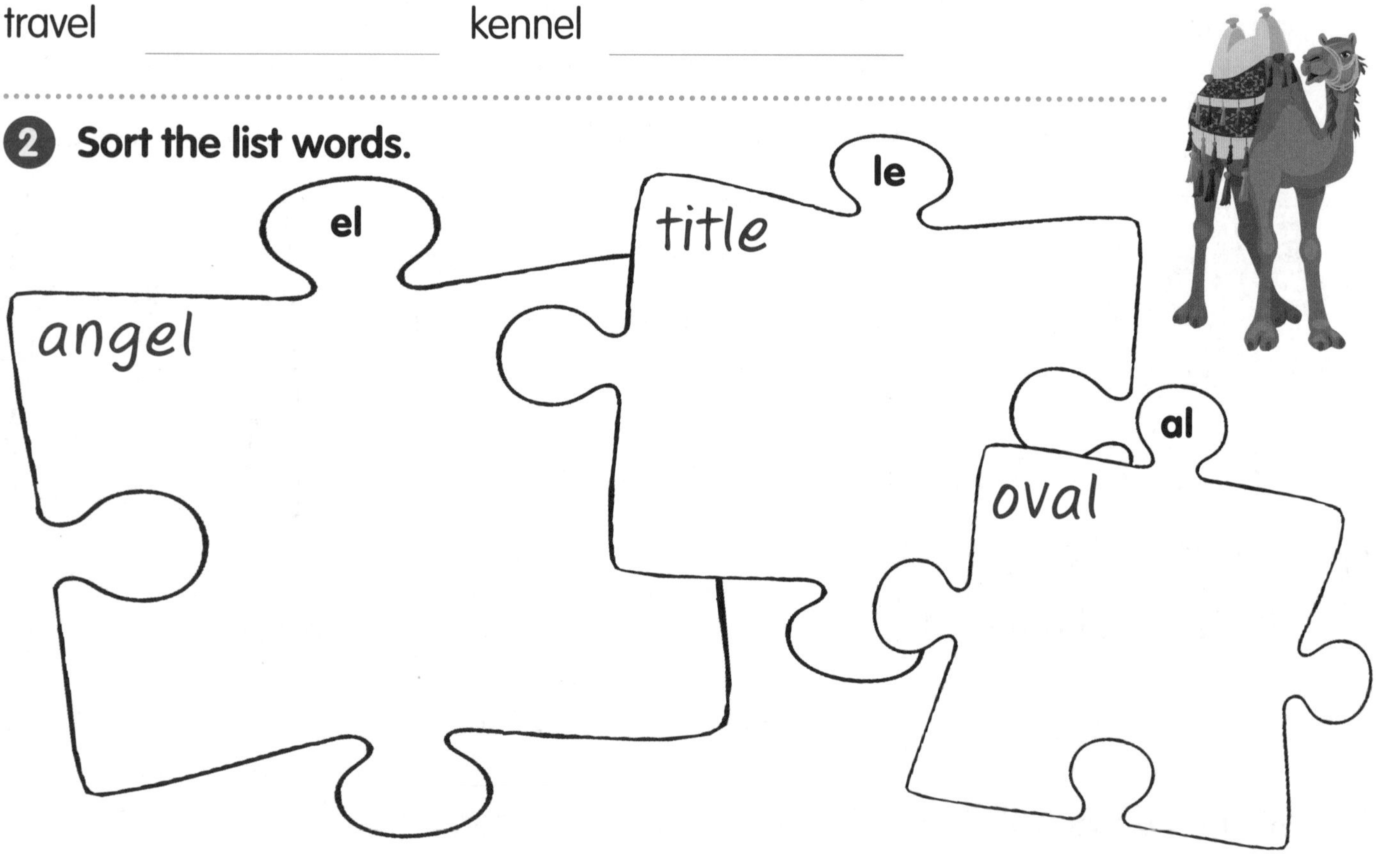

3 Write the name for each.

a 

n ____________

b 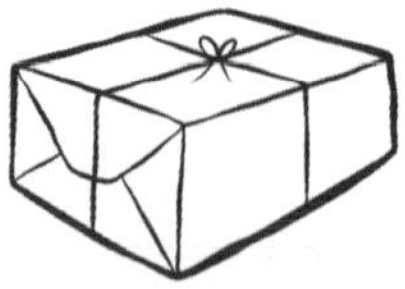

p ____________

c 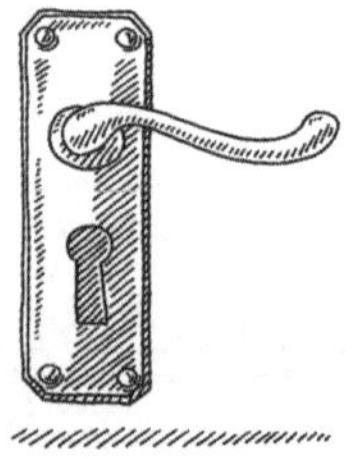

h ____________

d 

k ____________

L.2.2 Demonstrate command of the conventions of standard English capitalization, punctuation, and spelling when writing.

Endings: le, el, al

1 Underline the spelling mistake. Write it correctly.

a My grandparents sent me a parcal in the mail. ______

b I jumped over the puddel. ______

c I used a towl to dry off after my swim. ______

d You can see her dimpl when she smiles. ______

e We often travl overseas on our vacations. ______

Challenge words

2 Copy each challenge word.

turtle	______	shovel	______
buckle	______	cereal	______
people	______	capital	______
enamel	______	hospital	______
double	______	possible	______

3 Color the correct word.

a Dad told us all to [buckle] [buckal] our seatbelts.

b I helped [shovle] [shovel] mulch onto the garden.

c We ate [cerele] [cereal] for breakfast.

d Lots of [people] [peopel] live in the city.

4 Word clues. Which challenge word matches?

a twice the amount ______

b a place where sick people are cared for ______

c a reptile with a soft body and hard shell ______

Periods and question marks

A **sentence** is a group of words that makes complete sense. All sentences start with a capital letter. Sentences that tell something end with a period (.); e.g., Ollie is reading. Sentences that ask something end with a question mark (?); e.g., What is Ollie doing?

1 Fill in the missing punctuation.

a Joseph is writing a story

b What is in the bucket

c When does the show start

d Layla is helping her mother

e Where are my shoes

f The children are playing with their toys

g My friend has a new skateboard

h Which bag is yours

2 Write a sentence that tells what the boy is doing.

____

____

3 Write a question for this picture.

____

____

L.2.2 Demonstrate command of the conventions of standard English capitalization, punctuation, and spelling when writing.

Week 13 Day 1 **Comprehension**

The Dog and His Reflection

Visualization

Good readers imagine pictures when they read a text. This is called visualizing.

Looking for key words in the text helps you create the images.

Read the passage.

Circle words that **describe** the **bone**.

Box **where** the dog was going.

Underline **who** gave the dog the bone.

A dog had a fresh, meaty bone, which a butcher had thrown to him. He was heading home with his wonderful bone, as fast as he could go.

Circle the correct answer.

1. **What** did the butcher throw?

   a a bone b a biscuit c a treat d a ball

2. Which **key word** describes the dog's feelings about the bone?

   a fast b wonderful c butcher d thrown

3. Which two words help us **visualize** the bone?

   a butcher b meaty c wonderful d fresh

4. Which words help us **visualize** the dog's speed?

   a wonderful bone b meaty bone
   c thrown to him d as fast as he could go

The Dog and His Reflection

Read the passage.

As the dog crossed a bridge over a pond, he looked down and saw himself reflected in the quiet water. The image was like looking in a mirror.

But the dog thought he saw a real dog carrying another bone—a bone much bigger than his! Without thinking, the dog dropped his bone and leaped at the dog in the pond.

Circle what the **dog saw**.

Underline a word that **describes the water**.

1. **Where** did the dog see himself?

   a in the ocean b in a waterfall c in a pond d in a swimming pool

2. Which words helped you **visualize** the water?

   ____

3. **What** did the dog see?

   a a mirror b a bigger dog c a bigger bone d his reflection

4. **Where** can you see your own reflection?

   ____

5. **What** would the dog's reflection have looked like in the water?

   ____

RL.2.3 Describe how characters in a story respond to major events and challenges.

Digraph: wh

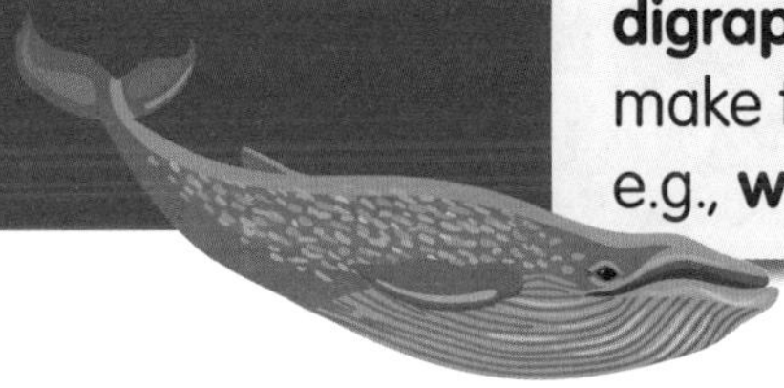

Two letters that make a single sound are called a **digraph**. The letters **wh** make the **single sound w**; e.g., **wh**isper, **wh**ip.

1 Copy each list word.

war ______	whip ______	worm ______
was ______	which ______	whale ______
wipe ______	witch ______	wheat ______
went ______	white ______	wheel ______
when ______	where ______	watch ______
what ______	world ______	while ______
wash ______	wall ______	

2 Underline the spelling mistake. Write the word correctly.

a People once believed the whorld was flat. ______

b She uses shampoo to whash her hair. ______

c The snowy owl has wite feathers. ______

d He dug a whorm out of the dirt. ______

e I couldn't tell wich pencil was mine. ______

3 The letter thief has left his bag behind! Put back the letters he stole.

a wo ___ ___ ___

b wi ___ ___ ___

c wh ___ ___

d wh ___ ___ ___

e w ___ ___ ___

f wa ___ ___

g wh ___ ___ ___

h we ___ ___

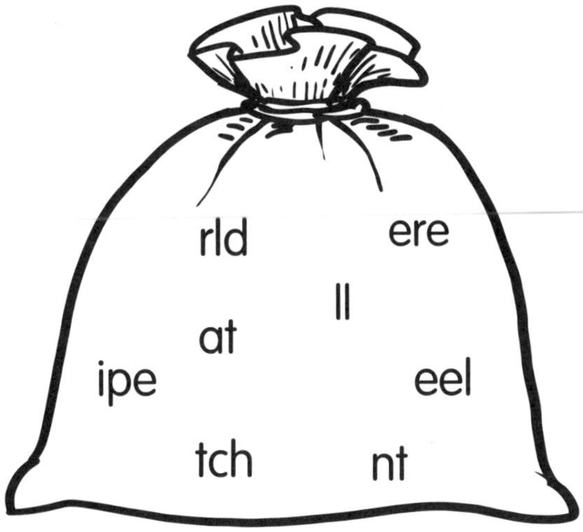

Digraph: wh

1 Write the name for each.

a

w ______

b

w ______

c
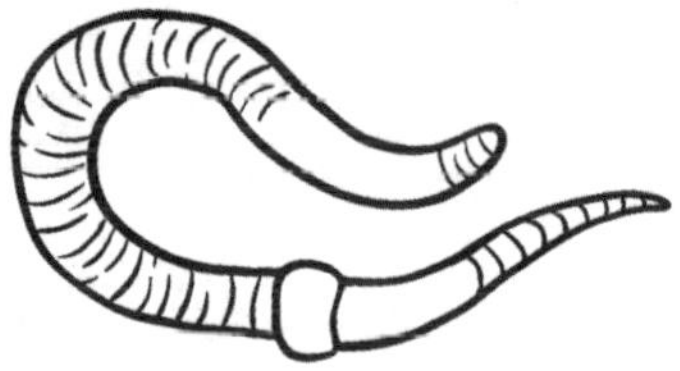
w ______

d
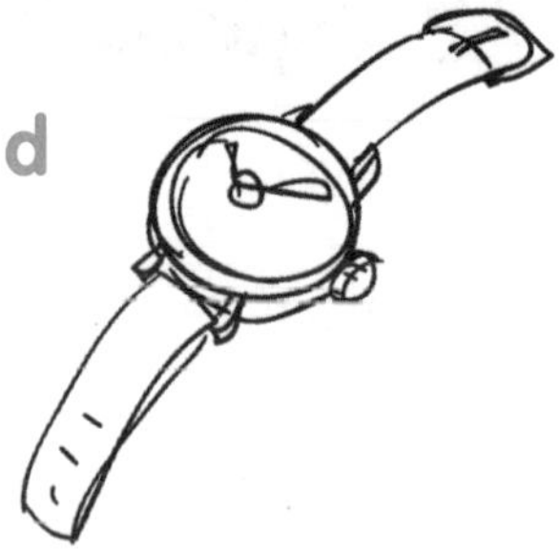
w ______

Challenge words

2 Copy each challenge word.

whistle ______	welcome ______
wagon ______	whether ______
whisk ______	weather ______
waste ______	wardrobe ______
whisker ______	wheeze ______

3 Complete each sentence with a challenge word.

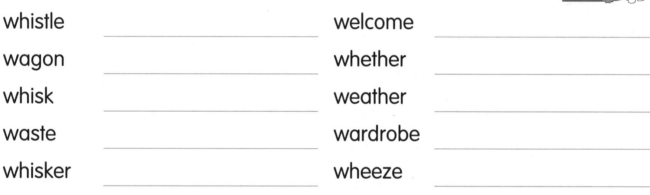

a She used a _ _ _ _ _ to whip the cream.

b The _ _ _ _ _ was pulled by two strong horses.

c I hung my clothes up in my _ _ _ _ _ _ _ _.

d The referee blew his _ _ _ _ _ _ _ to end the game.

e They have predicted stormy _ _ _ _ _ _ _ all weekend.

4 Make six words with the letters in wardrobe.

______ ______ ______

______ ______ ______

L.2.2 Demonstrate command of the conventions of standard English capitalization, punctuation, and spelling when writing.

Linking verbs

A **linking verb** does not show an action; e.g., I **am** happy. He **is** a tall boy. They **were** excited. We **have** a pet iguana.

1 Circle the correct verb.

a I smile when I (is, am) happy.

b The children (is, are) at the beach.

c I saw them when I (was, were) at the shop.

d The little girl is (be, being) naughty.

e My parents (was, were) very proud of me.

2 Complete each sentence with a verb from the box.

am is
are was
were

a This _______________ a kangaroo.

b Last week my puppy _______________ sick.

c These _______________ elephants.

d I _______________ a drummer.

e Yesterday the kittens _______________ playful.

3 Complete each sentence with a verb from the box.

have has had

a A tree _______________ branches and leaves.

b Birds _______________ feathers, beaks, and wings.

c Yesterday I _______________ pizza for dinner.

From Farms to You

Sequencing events

To identify the sequence of events in a text, look at numbers and words that give clues to the order in which things happen.

Read the passage.

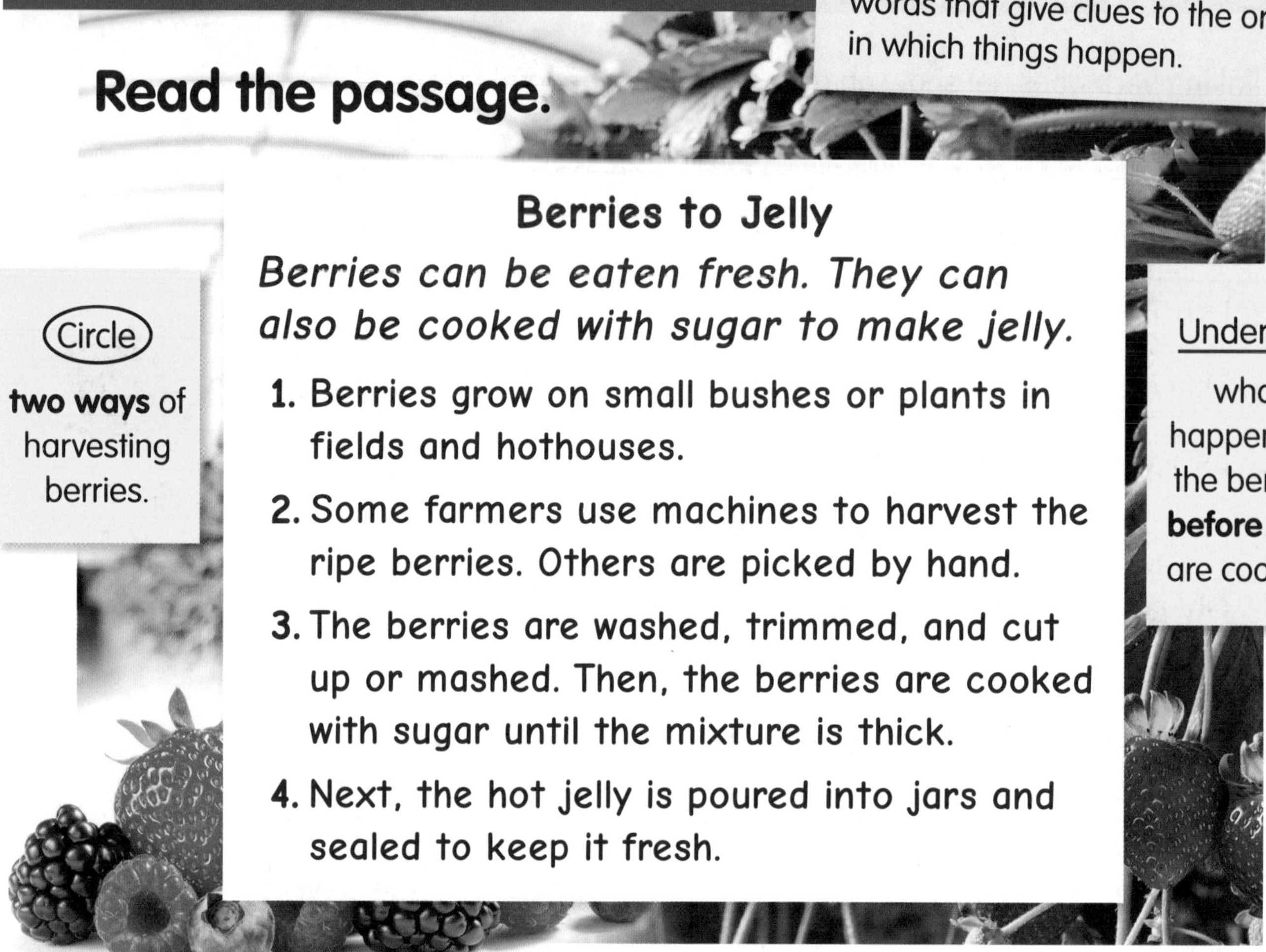

Circle **two ways** of harvesting berries.

Berries to Jelly

Berries can be eaten fresh. They can also be cooked with sugar to make jelly.

1. Berries grow on small bushes or plants in fields and hothouses.
2. Some farmers use machines to harvest the ripe berries. Others are picked by hand.
3. The berries are washed, trimmed, and cut up or mashed. Then, the berries are cooked with sugar until the mixture is thick.
4. Next, the hot jelly is poured into jars and sealed to keep it fresh.

Underline what happens to the berries **before** they are cooked.

1. What happens to the berries **before** they are harvested?

____

2. What happens to the berries **after** they are washed and mashed?

____

3. Where is the jelly poured **after** it is cooked?

____

4. What **text feature** tells you the steps must be done in order?

____

From Farms to You

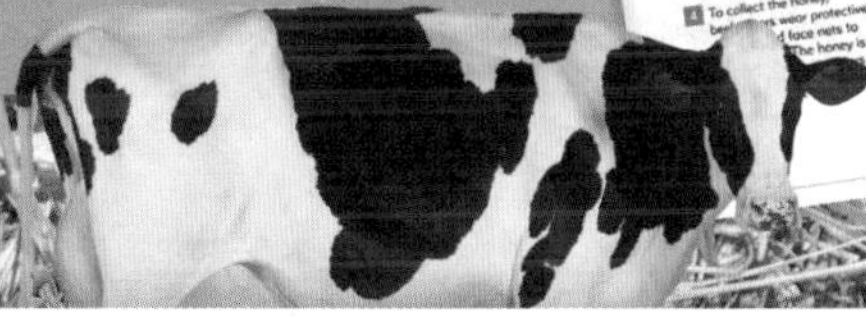

Read the passage.

Cows to Milk

First, the cows are taken to the milking shed.

________, they are milked using milking machines.

________, milk tankers take the milk to a factory where it is heated to kill any harmful bacteria.

________, the milk is put into bottles or cartons and kept refrigerated.

________, it is taken to stores and markets.

Finally
Then
Next
After this

1. Add the **time adverbs** to complete the passage.
2. Draw **the process** from cows in the milking shed to milk in the market.

Step 1	Step 2	Step 3
Step 6	Step 5	Step 4

Exceptions

Some words are tricky to spell because they contain letters that do not make their usual sounds; e.g., sure, again.

1 Copy each list word.

door	______	past	______	father	______
poor	______	child	______	pretty	______
after	______	hold	______	half	______
even	______	sure	______	hour	______
who	______	sugar	______	grass	______
again	______	prove	______	climb	______
bath	______	great	______		

2 Complete each sentence with a list word.

a I closed my bedroom d_ _ _ .

b He felt p_ _ _ after spending all his money.

c We watch television a_ _ _ _ dinner.

d Six and eight are e_ _ _ numbers.

e I h_ _ _ Mom's hand when crossing the road.

3 Which list word matches?

a			g			used to sweeten food and drinks
b			u			60 minutes
c		a				one of two equal parts
d					d	a young person

L.2.2 Demonstrate command of the conventions of standard English capitalization, punctuation, and spelling when writing.

Exceptions

1 **Write the list words from page 74 in alphabetical order.**

Challenge words

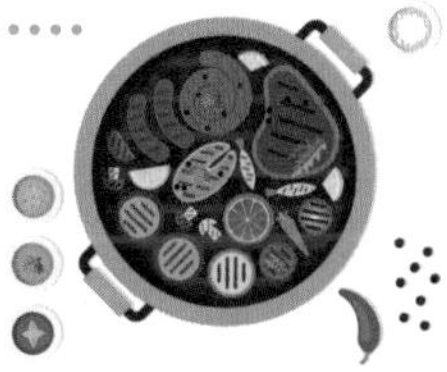

2 **Copy each challenge word.**

because
behind
steak
beautiful
clothes
would
should
whole
improve
everybody

3 **Underline the spelling mistake. Write the word correctly.**

a Dad grilled the stek and vegetables.

b He thought her painting was butiful.

c She ate a wole fruit bar.

d He wished everibody would just get along.

e We went shopping for new cloes.

4 **Use as many challenge words as possible to make a silly sentence.**

L.2.2 Demonstrate command of the conventions of standard English capitalization, punctuation, and spelling when writing.

Auxiliary verbs

Auxiliary verbs help **other verbs** do their work; e.g., I am **reading**. She is **drawing**. We are **singing**.

1 Complete each sentence with an auxiliary verb from the box.

has have am is are

a The dog __________ barking at the cat.

b I __________ making a card for my friend.

c Bella __________ found her other sock.

d The people __________ sitting in their seats.

e The children __________ finished their chores.

2 Complete the answers to the questions.

a What is Caleb doing?

Caleb is ______________________________

____

b What are the birds doing?

The birds are ____________________________

____

3 Underline the word that is wrong. Write it correctly.

a Michael have baked some cookies. __________

b The children is swimming in the lake. __________

c Lily and Phil was singing a song. __________

L.2.1 Demonstrate command of the conventions of standard English grammar and usage when writing or speaking.

Tools

Compare and contrast
This table compares and contrasts everyday tools people use. Look for **similarities** and **differences**.

Read the table.

Tool	Function	Powered by humans	Powered by electricity	Powered by battery
hammer	used to hammer nails, break rocks, and remove nails	✓	✗	✗
pen	used to write	✓	✗	✗
blender	used to mix foods and liquids	✗	✓	✗
calculator	used to do math	✗	✗	✓

1. Put a [✓] next to information that is true. Put a [✗] next to information that is false.

a [ ] Hammers and calculators are both powered by electricity.

b [ ] You must have a battery to use a pen.

c [ ] Batteries power calculators.

d [ ] Pens and hammers are powered by humans.

e [ ] A hammer and a pen have the same function.

f [ ] Blenders are powered by electricity.

Find the answer in the table.

2. Which tools are powered by humans? ______

3. Which tools are *not* powered by electricity? ______

4. Which tool is powered by battery? ______

5. Which tool is powered by electricity? ______

Tools

Read the passage.

Color tools schools used **from** the 1970s.

Box tools schools used **before** the 1970s.

1970s

Many new tools and gadgets became popular in the 1970s.

Prior to the 1970s, most schools used books, blackboards, and paper as educational tools.

By the 1970s, many schools had film projectors, record players, and tape recorders to help children learn.

By the late 1970s, people began to buy personal computers for their homes.

1. Complete the table using [✔] and [✘].

School Tool	Used before 1970	Used in the 1970s	Used today
Books			
Blackboards			
Paper and pencils			
Film projectors			
Record players			
Tape recorders			

2. Which tools were used **before 1970**?

3. Which tools were used before the 1970s and are **still used** in schools today?

RI.2.1 Ask and answer such questions as who, what, where, when, why, and how to demonstrate understanding of key details in a text.

Plurals: s, ves

A **plural** is more than one. For most nouns that end in f or fe, make them plural by changing f to v and **adding es**; e.g., leaf → lea**ves**.
Some nouns that end in f or fe just need an **s** to become plural; e.g., reef**s**.
For nouns that end in ve, just add **s** to make them plural; e.g., detective**s**.

1 Copy each list word.

lives	______	elves	______	loaves	______
puffs	______	waves	______	gloves	______
safes	______	stoves	______	giraffes	______
wives	______	leaves	______	cafes	______
reefs	______	sleeves	______	scarves	______
cliffs	______	olives	______	shelves	______
hives	______	wolves	______		

2 Write the singular and plural for each word.

a		______	______	
b		______	______	
c		______	______	
d		______	______	

3 Write the word as a plural.

a I wear (glove) ______ to keep my hands warm.

b We saw lots of (giraffe) ______ at the zoo.

c There are three (shelf) ______ in the closet.

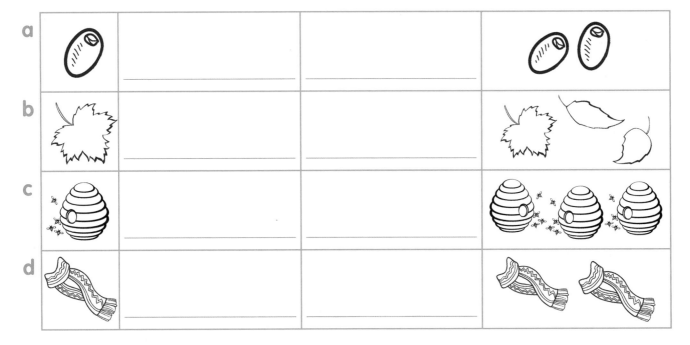

Plurals: s, ves

1 **Sort the list words from page 79.**

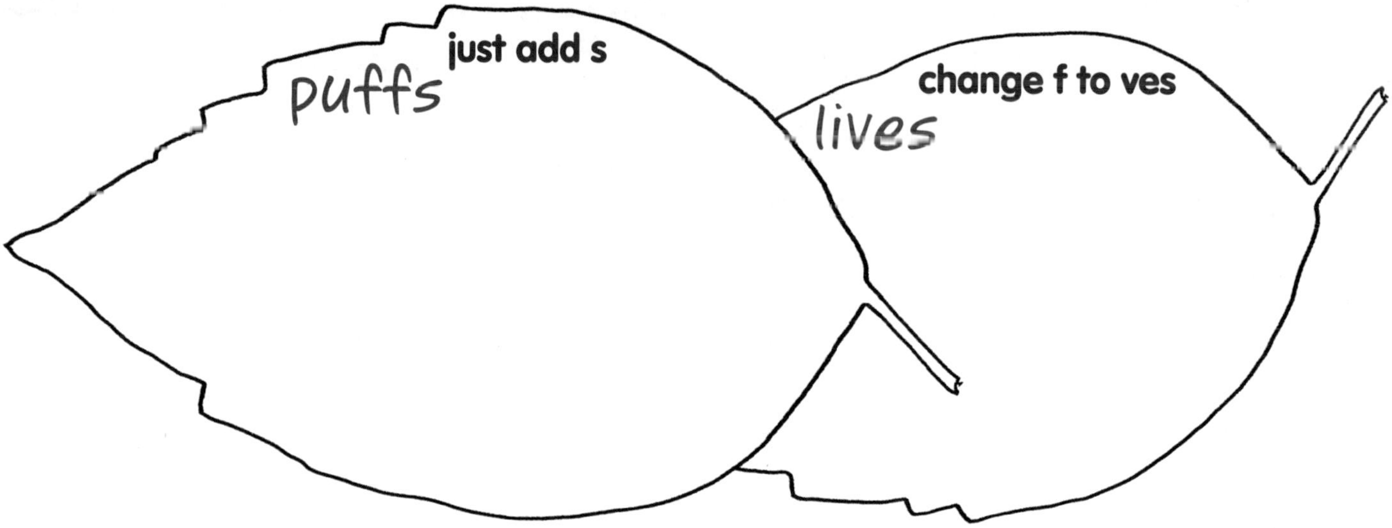

Challenge words

2 **Copy each challenge word.**

knives ______	calves ______
halves ______	grooves ______
sheaves ______	selves ______
thieves ______	flagstaffs ______
nerves ______	detectives ______

3 **Complete each sentence with a challenge word.**

a In the cutlery drawer we have spoons, forks, and ______.

b We saw lots of ______ with their mothers on the farm.

c My shoes have ______ on the bottom.

d I divided the orange into two ______.

4 **Use challenge words to make a very silly sentence.**

______

______

L.2.2 Demonstrate command of the conventions of standard English capitalization, punctuation, and spelling when writing.

Progressive tense

The **present progressive tense** shows that an action is happening now. It has the helping verbs **am**, **is**, or **are** before the main verb; e.g., I **am** speaking. They **are** cheering.
The **past progressive tense** shows that an action happened over a period of time. It has the helping verbs **was** and **were** before the main verb; e.g., I **was** speaking. They **were** cheering.

1 Sort the verbs.

was picking   is picking   are jogging   were jogging

Present progressive (happening now)	Past progressive (has happened)
______________________	______________________
______________________	______________________

2 Complete each sentence with a helping verb from the box.

a I ____________ writing a story.
b Danny ____________ eating his lunch.
c I ____________ helping my neighbor.
d We ____________ going on a bear hunt.

am
is
are

3 Cross out the word that is wrong. Write it correctly.

a I were making a card for my friend. ____________
b Luca are waiting for the train. ____________
c The girls was playing basketball. ____________
d The children is walking to the library. ____________

Transport

Compare and contrast
Look for **similarities** and **differences** between details in the text.

Read the passage.

Underline the **purpose** of transport.

Box types of **public transport**.

Color a **word** that means the same as **transport**.

Circle types of **private transport**.

Transport

Vehicles, such as cars, buses, trains, planes, and boats, transport us from one place to another.

Some people use transport to make short, daily trips to work or school. Others use it for longer journeys, such as a vacation or business trip overseas.

Public transport is designed for moving large groups of people. Buses, trains, trams, ferries, and planes are types of public transport. Private transport includes cars, motorcycles, and bicycles.

1. Complete the table about transport.

	Purpose	Examples
Private transport		
Public transport		

2. What does all transport do? ____________________

Transport

Read the passage.

Box **when** people began buying cars.

Underline **when** more roads appeared.

Color **why** Ford's cars were affordable.

Circle **how** road safety became an issue.

Cars

In the early 1900s, people began to buy their own cars. In 1908, Henry Ford began making cars on an assembly line. His factory made cars at a much faster rate. These mass-produced cars were cheaper to buy.

In the 1950s, many more people owned cars. More cars meant more roads. With more cars on the road, people started to think about car safety. The first seat belts strapped across the driver's lap.

1. Make a timeline about cars.

Early 1900s	**1908**	**1950s**

2. **When** were cars first mass produced?

a 1901–1910 b 1961–1970 c 1911–1920 d 1951–1960

3. **When** were more roads built?

a 1931–1940 b 1901–1910 c 1951–1960 d 1941–1950

Week 16 Day 3 Spelling

Long oo exceptions

Two letters that make a single sound are called a **digraph**. Many vowel combinations make an **oo sound**. The letters **ou, ui, oe, ue,** and **ew** all sometimes make an **oo sound**; e.g., s**ou**p, s**ui**t, can**oe**, bl**ue**, bl**ew**. Sometimes **the single vowel u** makes an **oo sound**; e.g., fl**u**.

1 Copy each list word.

you		rude		threw	
fruit		grew		blew	
shoe		clue		chew	
blue		crew		screw	
flew		suit		prune	
soup		group		ruby	
true		truth			

2 Name.

a

s

b
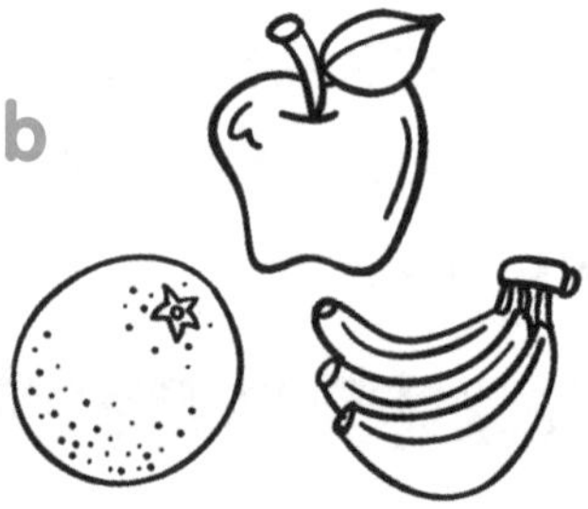
f

c

s

d

s

3 Match the clue to a list word.

a		u				a deep red gem
b			o			something worn on your foot
c	f					grown on plants
d		r			e	a dried plum
e			u			the color of the sky

L.2.2 Demonstrate command of the conventions of standard English capitalization, punctuation, and spelling when writing.

Long oo exceptions

1 Write the missing letters to complete the list words.

a sc__ __ __ b cl__ __ c gr__ __

d cr__ __ e bl__ __ f fl__ __

g ch__ __ h th__ __ __ i s__ __p

Challenge words

2 Copy each challenge word.

bruise	________	should	________
bluish	________	through	________
cruise	________	canoe	________
would	________	cashew	________
could	________	gruesome	________

3 Color the correct word.

a I [could] [cowld] not stop listening to her new song.

b I screamed as my brother capsized our [canoo] [canoe].

c I had a [groosome] [gruesome] scrape on my knee.

d The train sped [throo] [through] the tunnel.

4 Complete each sentence with a challenge word.

a I had a large ________ on my leg after falling over.

b I had a packet of ________ nuts for my morning snack.

c I wish that I ________ fly like a bird.

d Mom told me that I ________ go and clean my room.

Future tense

Future tense verbs show that an action will happen in the future. The future tense is formed by writing the helping verb **will** in front of the main verb; e.g., Declan **will** make his bed later. You can also write the words **am going to**, **is going to**, or **are going to** in front of the verb; e.g., They **are going to** rest this afternoon.

1 Use the pictures to answer the questions.

a Where will you climb?

I will climb ______________________________

b How are you going to travel?

I am going to travel ______________________________

c When will they arrive?

They will arrive ______________________________

2 Complete each sentence.

a You ____________ miss your train if you don't hurry.

b My father ____________ going to fetch me later.

c I ____________ going to meet them at the park.

d Alex is ____________ to invite me to his party.

e The dentist is going ____________ clean my teeth.

3 Write each sentence in the future tense.

a Yesterday I bought a new model plane.

Tomorrow ______________________________

b Last week I visited my cousins in Hawaii.

Next week ______________________________

L.2.1 Demonstrate command of the conventions of standard English grammar and usage when writing or speaking.

Postcards

Making connections

Good readers know how to make connections in a text. They link words, ideas, and events to themselves, things they have read, and real world events.

Read the postcard.

Underline **when** they went to the zoo.

Box **what** they saw at the zoo.

Color **who** went to the zoo.

Circle **what** they ate at the zoo.

Dear Mom,

Today we got up really early and went to the zoo. It was huge! The giraffes had lots of room and the lions hid in the bushes. Dad pretended to be a mountain goat. We bought ice creams after lunch. Boo-boo had chocolate and I had vanilla. Dad carried us when we got really tired. See you tomorrow!

Love, T

xx

1 Make connections to the text. [✓] for yes. [✗] for no.

a [ ] Have you ever got up really early?

b [ ] Have you ever been to the zoo?

c [ ] Have you ever seen a mountain goat?

d [ ] Have you ever had ice cream after lunch?

2 Write about one of your connections to the text.

____

____

____

Postcards

AIR-MAIL

Read the postcard.

Underline **when** they arrived in Paris.

Box **what** they thought of Paris.

Color **who** is in Paris.

Circle **where** they went in Paris.

Dear Anna and Janek,

We arrived in Paris yesterday afternoon. Last night we went up to the top of the Eiffel Tower. The city was all lit up and so pretty. Today we went to three art galleries, so I have sore feet! What have you been doing?

Love, Vicky and Sean

PLACE STAMP HERE

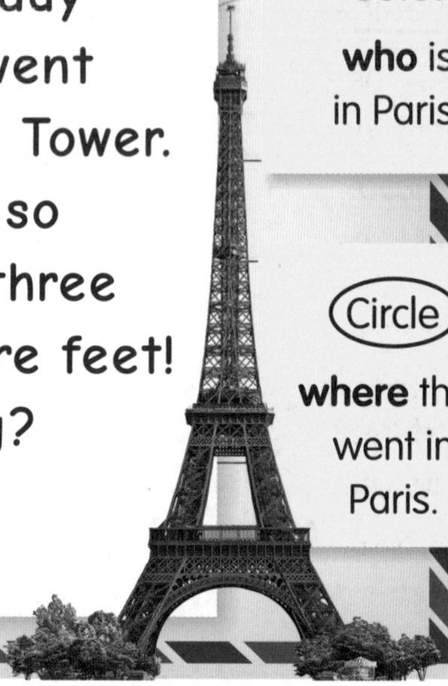

Use your knowledge to answer questions about postcards.

1. **What** is a postcard? ______________________________

2. **Why** do people write postcards? ______________________________

____

3. **What** information do people give in a postcard? ______________________________

____

4. Imagine you are somewhere else. Write a postcard to yourself.

____

____

____

RI.2.1 Ask and answer such questions as who, what, where, when, why, and how to demonstrate understanding of key details in a text.

Suffixes: ful, less

Adding the **suffix ful** to a noun or verb turns it into an adjective; e.g., pain**ful**, or another noun; e.g., mouth**ful**.

Adding the **suffix less** to a noun or verb turns it into an adjective; e.g., help**less**.

1 Copy each list word.

awful		handful		grateful	
useless		joyful		powerful	
helpful		playful		spiteful	
careless		mouthful		cheerful	
spoonful		graceful		truthful	
plateful		thankful		harmless	
restless		forgetful			

2 Sort the list words.

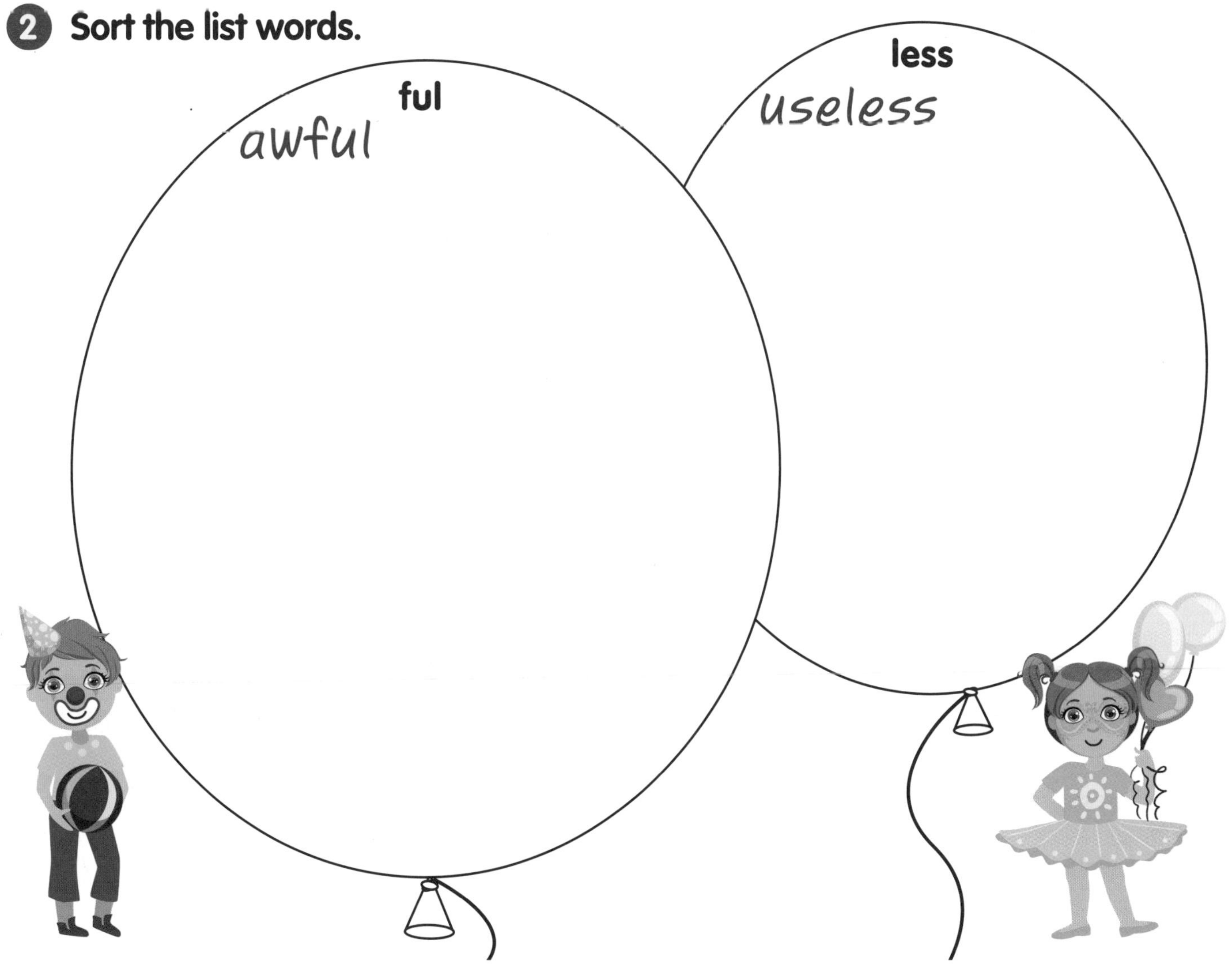

Suffixes: ful, less

1 Underline the spelling mistake. Write it correctly.

a She would only eat a spoonfull of the soup. ____________

b Mom gave us each a platefull of pasta. ____________

c His careles mistake got him into trouble. ____________

d Dad told us he wanted a truthfull answer. ____________

Challenge words

2 Copy each challenge word.

beautiful ____________	merciful ____________
wonderful ____________	plentiful ____________
colorless ____________	houseful ____________
delightful ____________	peaceful ____________
faithful ____________	disgraceful ____________

3 Complete each sentence.

a We had a p____________ supply of food.

b Water is a c____________ liquid.

c Coach said I had made w____________ progress this season.

d We were punished for our d____________ behavior.

4 Use as many challenge words as possible to make a silly sentence.

L.2.2 Demonstrate command of the conventions of standard English capitalization, punctuation, and spelling when writing.

Reflexive pronouns

Reflexive pronouns refer, or "reflect", back to a noun or pronoun; e.g., **I** made **myself** noodles. The reflexive pronouns are **myself, yourself, himself, herself, itself, ourselves, yourselves, themselves.**

1 Draw lines to match the pronouns.

Singular	
I	himself
you	itself
he	myself
she	yourself
it	herself

Plural	
we	themselves
you	ourselves
them	yourselves

2 Circle the correct word.

a The man told (yourself, himself) not to panic.

b Our cat cleans (ourselves, itself) with its tongue.

c The babies feed (yourselves, themselves) with spoons.

d We are watching (yourselves, ourselves) on television.

e My father blamed (themselves, himself) for the mistake.

3 Complete each sentence with a reflexive pronoun.

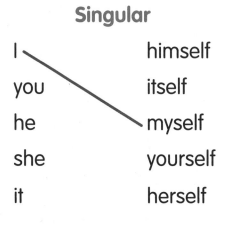

a She made it for ____________________ and no one else.

b They looked at ____________________ in the mirror.

c We helped ____________________ to more ice cream.

d Dad hurt ____________________ when he slipped on the banana skin.

e You will burn ____________________ if you get too close to the fire.

Signs

Word study

Good readers use clues in the text and their own knowledge to work out word meanings. It helps to understand the author's intention.

Read the signs.

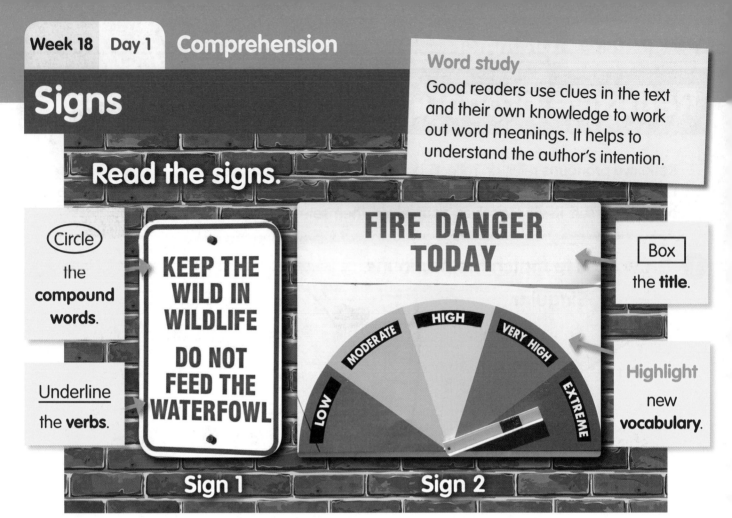

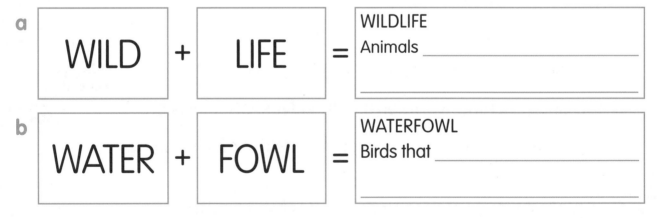

Sign 1

1 Complete these definitions.

a WILD + LIFE = WILDLIFE
Animals ______________________
____

b WATER + FOWL = WATERFOWL
Birds that ______________________
____

Sign 2

2 Complete these sentences.

a The highest fire danger warning is ______________________.

b Extreme means ______________________.

c People feel safest when the fire danger is ______________________.

RI.2.4 Determine the meaning of words and phrases in a text relevant to a grade 2 topic or subject area.

Signs

Read the sign.

1. **What** does fragile mean? ______

2. Which **clues** helped you to know this? ______

______

3. **What** do the pictures tell you? ______

______

4. **Name** three things that are fragile. ______

______

5. **Where** would you expect to see this sign? ______

______

______

RI.2.4 Determine the meaning of words and phrases in a text relevant to a grade 2 topic or subject area.

Silent letters

Some words have a **silent letter** at the beginning. We say the second letter.

Words that are spelled with **k**n or **g**n at the start, begin with the sound n; e.g., **k**nee, **g**nome.

Words that start with **w**r, begin with the sound r; e.g., **w**rinkle.

1 Copy each list word.

know		
gnat	write	gnome
knee	knot	wrong
wrap	knife	wrote
knit	knock	wrist
knob	kneel	gnash
knew	knelt	
wreck	knack	

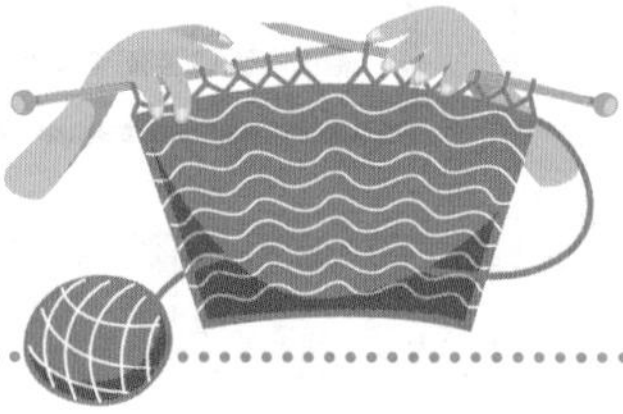

2 Name.

a  gn

b  kn

c  kn

d  wr

3 Fit words into the blocks.

a		r		t	
b	k				l
c	g			s	

L.2.2 Demonstrate command of the conventions of standard English capitalization, punctuation, and spelling when writing.

Silent letters

1 Complete each sentence with a list word.

a I heard a __________ at the front door.

b I __________ down to tie my shoelaces.

c My big brother had trouble brushing the ________ out of his hair.

d I hooked the bracelet around my __________.

Challenge words

2 Copy each challenge word.

written		wrestle	
wreckage		knight	
knuckle		known	
wrinkle		gnaw	
wriggle		knead	

3 Complete each sentence with a challenge word.

a I could not get the ring over my ______________.

b I watched the worm ______________ in the dirt.

c The brave ____________ rode away on his horse.

d The ________________ from the storm took weeks to clean up.

e The baker must __________ the dough before putting it in the oven.

4 Use as many challenge words as possible to make a silly story.

Periods and exclamation points

Sentences that tell something end with a period. Sentences that express a **strong feeling**—like fear, surprise, or excitement—sometimes end with an exclamation point (!); e.g., You scared me! If a sentence expresses a strong feeling and it starts with **What** or **How**, it always ends with an exclamation point; e.g., **What** an amazing day that was! **How** good was that!

1 **Fill in the missing periods and exclamation points.**

a Please take a ball and a mitt

b What a good child he is

c How exciting was that exhibit

d I gave Ben one of my trading cards

e I've invited Eva and Claire to my party

f I can't wait to ride my new bike

2 **Change these sentences to exclamations. Start each sentence with How.**

That is very good. *How good is that!*

a That was brilliant. ______________________

b This is exciting. ______________________

3 **Change these sentences to exclamations. Start each sentence with What.**

That was a great story. *What a great story that was!*

a That is a cute puppy.

____

b That was an exciting ride.

____

L.2.2 Demonstrate command of the conventions of standard English capitalization, punctuation, and spelling when writing.

Spelling

Use this review to test your knowledge. It has three parts—**Spelling**, **Grammar**, and **Comprehension**. If you're unsure of an answer, go back and read the rules and generalizations in the blue boxes.

You have learned about:

- plurals with y
- digraph: wh
- long oo exceptions
- j sound
- exceptions
- suffixes: ful, less
- endings: le, el, al
- plurals: s, ves
- silent letters

1 Complete each word with *le, el,* or *al.* 3 marks

a tow__ __ b ov__ __ c pudd__ __

2 Which word completes the sentence? 1 mark

Eli put a __________ of mashed potato on his plate.

a spoons b spoonless c spoonful d spooned

3 Complete each word with *wh, kn, gn,* or *wr.* 4 marks

a __ __ob b __ __ist c __ __ale d __ __ash

4 Which word completes the sentence? 1 mark

I want to __________ Stony Man Mountain in Virginia.

a climb b climbed c climbing d climbs

5 Complete. 1 mark

a one party, two __________

b one ruby, two __________

c one scarf, two __________

d one café, two __________

Your score

___
10

Grammar

You have learned about:

- action verbs
- linking verbs
- future tense
- present and past tense
- auxiliary verbs
- reflexive pronouns
- periods and question marks
- progressive tense
- periods and exclamation points

1 **Color the action verb in each circle.** 2 marks

a run is

b has catch

2 **Underline the word that is wrong. Write it correctly.** 2 marks

a Last night I cook dinner. ______________

b Last week we wash our car. ______________

3 **Fill in the missing punctuation.** 2 marks

a Where are we going

b We are going to the beach

4 **Complete each sentence with a linking verb from the box.** 3 marks

am have is

a It ______________ very hot today.

b I ______________ excited about getting a dog.

c The pirates ______________ treasure on their ship.

Grammar

5 Complete each sentence with an auxiliary verb. 2 marks

am

are

a I __________ putting away my books.

b The children __________ cheering for their team.

6 Cross out the word that is wrong. Write it correctly. 2 marks

a I were waiting for the bus. __________

b Jack are eating his sandwiches. __________

7 Fill in the missing verbs in these future tense sentences. 2 marks

a You __________ fall if you're not careful.

b I __________ going to buy tickets for the concert.

8 Complete each sentence with a reflexive pronoun. 3 marks

yourself herself themselves

a The children helped __________ to sandwiches.

b She made __________ a hot chocolate.

c You might see __________ on TV.

9 Fill in the missing punctuation. 2 marks

a How good was that book

b I'd like to read that book again

Your score

/20

Dolphins and Porpoises

Read the passage and then use the comprehension skills you have learned to answer the questions.

There are 31 species of dolphin and six species of porpoise.

Some dolphin species, such as the bottlenose dolphin, live in oceans. Others live in coastal waters and rivers. Porpoises, such as the harbor porpoise, live in coastal waters.

Dolphins and porpoises eat fish and squid. They breathe through a blowhole, which closes when the animal is underwater. They have flippers and streamlined bodies. All dolphins and porpoises have a dorsal fin, except the finless porpoise.

Dolphins and porpoises mostly live and hunt in groups called pods. Pods protect dolphins from predators. If a shark attacks, bottlenose dolphins fiercely defend their pod. They ram the shark's soft belly with their snouts.

1 How many species of dolphin are there? 1 mark — LITERAL

a thirty-six b thirty-one c thirteen d thirty

2 Where do dolphins and porpoises live? 1 mark — LITERAL

a on land b underground

c in water d on the land and in water

Dolphins and Porpoises

3 What helps dolphins and porpoises swim fast? 1 mark INFERENTIAL

a their flippers and streamlined bodies
b their blowholes
c their dorsal fins
d their bottle-shaped noses

4 Which statement is true? Dolphins and porpoises eat … 1 mark LITERAL

a seaweed and seagrass.
b sharks and whales.
c fish and squid.
d other dolphins and porpoises.

5 Where do dolphins and porpoises breathe? 1 mark INFERENTIAL

a below the surface of the water
b above the surface of the water
c deep underwater
d on rocks and beaches

6 What is a group of dolphins called? 1 mark LITERAL

a a herd
b a flock
c an army
d a pod

7 Which animals prey on dolphins and porpoises? 1 mark LITERAL

a turtles
b seals
c sharks
d clown fish

8 Which word in the text shows that dolphins can be aggressive? VOCABULARY

a fiercely
b protect
c defend
d finless

9 In the text, which words can be used in place of *ram*? 1 mark VOCABULARY

a push around
b squeeze hard
c pull apart
d crash into

10 Which part of the dolphin is its snout? 1 mark INFERENTIAL

a the top of the head
b the mouth and nose
c the side of the head
d the tail

Your score ☐ / 10

Your Review 2 Scores

Spelling		Grammar		Comprehension		Total
☐ / 10	+	☐ / 20	+	☐ / 10	=	☐ / 40

Artrageous

Think marks

To understand what you are reading, you can use **special marks**. These help you see the parts you understand, and any new vocabulary.

- *I can see this part*
- **W** *What's this word?*
- ✓ *I understand this part*

Read the passage.

Color **who** is in the story.

Circle **what** Luke imagined.

Box **what** Sophie imagined.

Underline **what** Aunt Stella imagined.

Imagine This, Imagine That

"It's easy. One person starts imagining something that doesn't exist, say a flying car, and the next person has to add to it," said Luke.

"So you could imagine a flying car shaped like a fish," said Aunt Stella.

Sophie understood. "And the flying car shaped like a fish could spray fireworks from its wheels."

Circle the correct answer.

1. **What** does Luke imagine?
   - a a flying car
   - b a fish in a flying car
   - c a flying car that can swim
   - d a fish spraying fireworks
2. **Who** is in the story?
   - a a fish, a flying car, Aunt Stella
   - b Aunt Stella, Luke, Sophie
   - c a fish named Fireworks, Aunt Sophie, a car
   - d Luke, a flying car, Spray
3. **Which** word could replace *understood* in this story?
   - a hugged
   - b won
   - c proved
   - d followed

RL.2.1 Ask and answer such questions as who, what, where, when, why, and how to demonstrate understanding of key details in a text.

Artrageous

Read the passage.

Use Think Marks to help you understand the passage.

Box **what** Sophie collected.

Circle **what** Sophie liked about the shells.

Color **what** Sophie liked best.

Art Eyes

"Look out for colors, patterns, shapes, textures, and shadows that catch your attention. Draw them in your journal and collect as much treasure as you can!" Aunt Stella cried.

Sophie liked the shapes and colors of the shells. She collected lots of shells of all shapes, sizes, colors, and patterns.

Sophie also rubbed some rock textures into her journal and drew a rough sketch of the beach. But her most precious find was a piece of blue, weathered glass.

1. **What** did Sophie collect? ______________________
2. **What** did Sophie draw? ______________________
3. **Which** word helps you understand that Sophie *valued* the piece of glass?

____

4. Write about a time you found something precious.

____

____

____

____

Week 19 Day 3 Spelling

Suffixes: er, est

When we compare two nouns, we often add the **suffix er** to an adjective; e.g., short**er**. When we compare MORE than two nouns, we often add the **suffix est** to an adjective; e.g., loud**est**.

1 Copy each list word.

paler ______	neatest ______	prouder ______
duller ______	cuter ______	steeper ______
nicer ______	newest ______	fullest ______
fewer ______	whiter ______	sharper ______
finest ______	coldest ______	smallest ______
later ______	thickest ______	clearest ______
loudest ______	fresher ______	

2 Sort the list words.

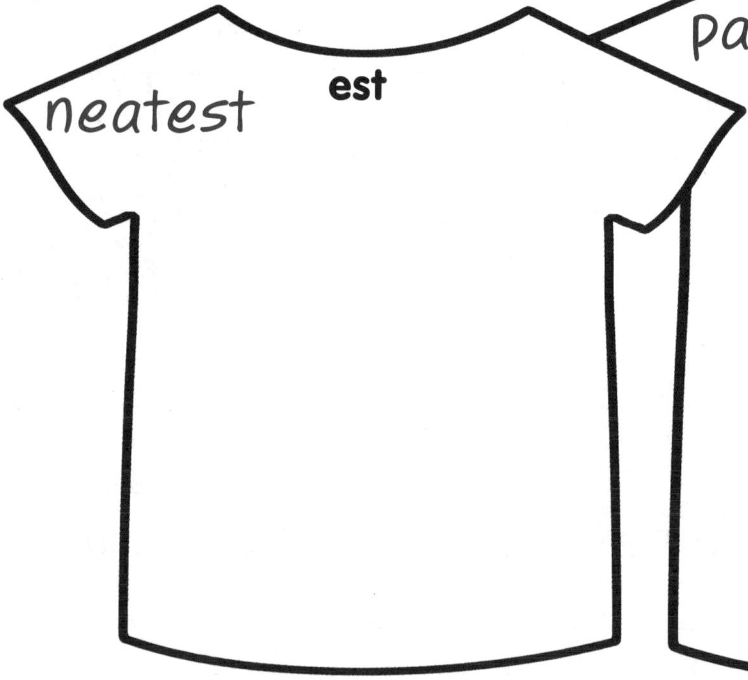

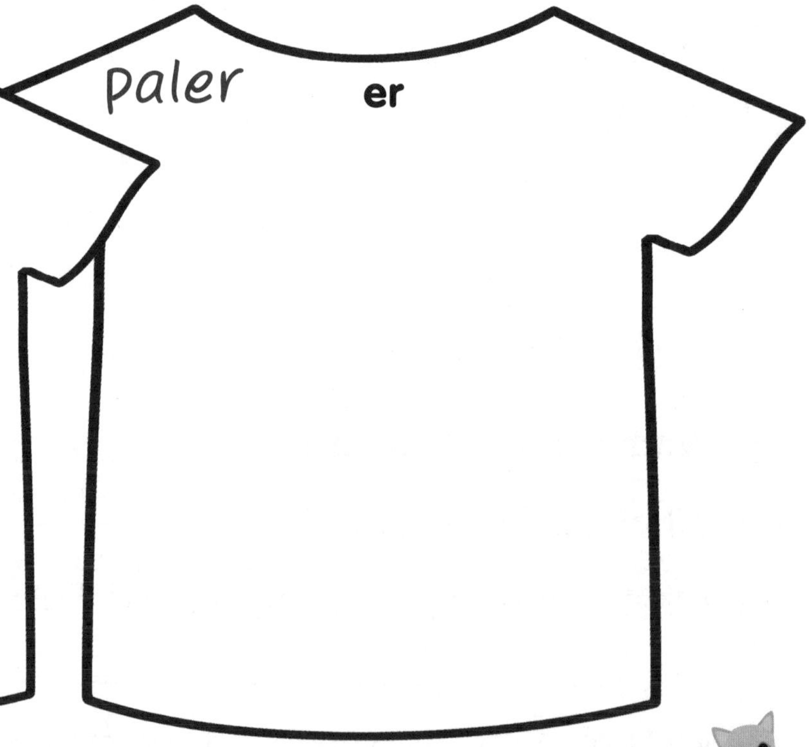

3 Underline the spelling mistake. Write the word correctly.

a Kay chose the smalest kitten from the litter. ______

b I think my puppy is coouter than my dog. ______

c The mountain was a lot steper than the hill. ______

L.2.2 Demonstrate command of the conventions of standard English capitalization, punctuation, and spelling when writing.

Suffixes: er, est

1 Match these list words to their word shapes.

neatest fresher paler sharper nicer

a 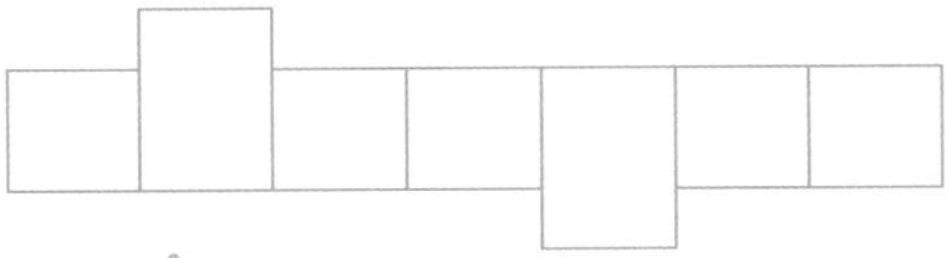

b 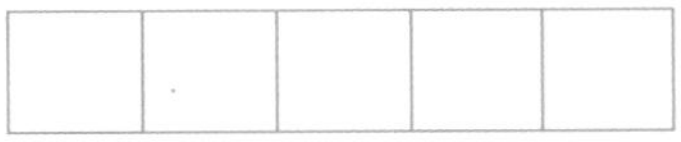

c 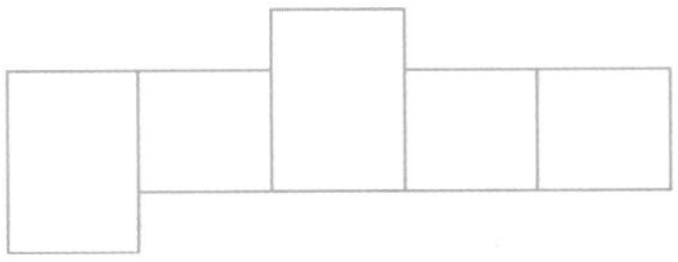

d 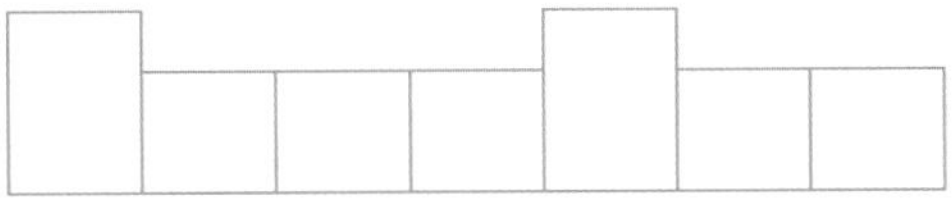

e 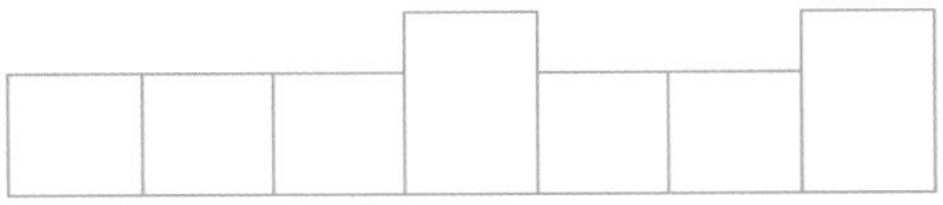

Challenge words

2 Copy each challenge word.

higher ______	straighter ______
bluer ______	quietest ______
narrowest ______	younger ______
gentler ______	looser ______
brightest ______	fiercer ______

3 Color the correct word.

a I am [youngest] [younger] than my brother.

b The sun is [brightst] [brightest] at midday.

c Her hair is a lot [straighter] [straightest] than my hair.

d The [fiercer] [fierceer] warrior won the duel.

e The blue bird was [higher] [highest] than the orange bird.

4 Use as many challenge words as possible to make silly sentences.

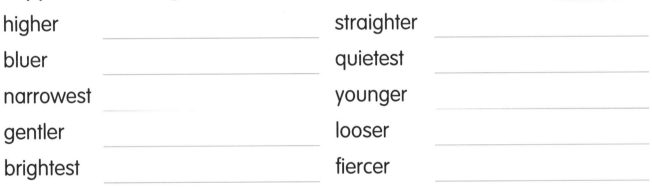

______

______

______

Possessive nouns

Apostrophes (') are used to show **ownership**. If something belongs to someone or something, the name of the owner is followed by 's; e.g., That is Jack's pet rabbit.

1 Circle the possessive noun.

a the cat's fur
b the bird's wings
c Ruby's pencil
d Liam's jacket
e the baby's toy
f the book's cover
g Sam's pencil
h the frog's legs
i Mandy's party
j the monkey's tail

2 In each pair, check [✓] the sentence that has the correct punctuation.

a My mother's purse is on the table. ☐
b My mothers' purse is on the table. ☐

c The birds nest is on the branch. ☐
d The bird's nest is on the branch. ☐

e My rabbit's fur is very soft. ☐
f My rabbits fur is very soft. ☐

3 Fill in the missing apostrophes.

a Alex is wearing Joses mitt.
b Dads car is in the garage.
c My grandpas glasses are on the table.
d The boys lunch is in his bag.
e The childs T-shirt is covered in mud.
f Bens kitten is very playful.

The World's Longest Toenail

Making inferences

Use **clues** in the text to make an inference.

The clues help you find the answers that are hiding in the text.

Read the passage.

Circle **who** was trapped.

Underline **what** trapped the person.

Box **what** the people were doing.

Color **how** Jake felt.

Smelly and Stuck

Jake's toenail went PING! Jake spun around like a corkscrew. And there he stuck.

Everybody pushed and shoved. People with cameras took photos. People with notebooks asked questions.

"What does it feel like to be trapped by your toenail, Jake? they asked.

The sacks were full of fertilizer. The longest toenail in the world was no fun anymore.

Circle the correct answer.

1. **Which** best describes how Jake was feeling?
   a confused b unhappy c giddy d happy
2. Which **clue** tells you this?
   a "What does it feel like to be trapped by your toenail, Jake?"
   b The sacks were full of fertilizer.
   c The longest toenail in the world was no fun anymore.
3. What **inference** can we make about Jake?
   a Jake is the center of attention.
   b Jake wants the longest toenail in the world.
   c Jake likes having his photo taken.

4. What **inference** can we make about the situation?
   a There were a few people there. b There were a lot of people there.
   c There was one person there.

The World's Longest Toenail

Read the passage.

(Circle) **what** was growing.

Color **where** the toenail grew.

Underline the speed of Jake's growing toenail.

Sam's Cool Idea

The longest toenail in the world was growing.

Longer and wider and taller! And it was growing FAST!

It curled three times round his body. It shot past his ears. It twisted over his head. It snaked up past the diving board.

Jake gasped as his toenail snaked and grew. As big as himself ... as tall as a tree ... as big as a house ... as tall as a crane.

1. **Draw** Jake and his enormous toenail.

2. How would you **feel** about having a very long toenail?

3. We can **infer** that Jake was worried. What is the clue?

RL.2.3 Describe how characters in a story respond to major events and challenges.

Week 20 Day 3 **Spelling**

Homophones

> **Homophones** are words that sound the same but are spelled differently and have different meanings; e.g., toe, tow.

1 Copy each list word.

sale	______	steal	______	sight	______
sail	______	flee	______	site	______
meet	______	flea	______	toe	______
meat	______	hole	______	tow	______
plane	______	whole	______	rain	______
plain	______	pray	______	rein	______
steel	______	prey	______		

2 Circle the right word.

a		flea flee	b	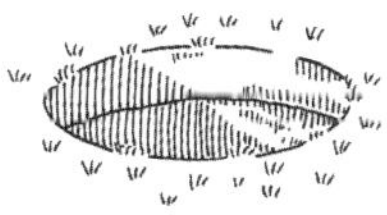	hole whole	c	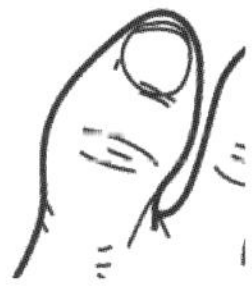	tow toe
d	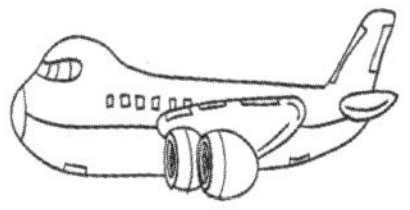	plane plain	e		sail sale	f		rein rain
g	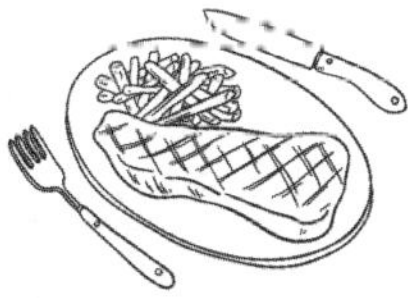	meet meat	h		steel steal			

3 Write the missing word.

a The ______ landed safely at the airport.

b The mole dug a deep ______ in the dirt.

c We watched the boats ______ past the harbor.

d I bought a box of old toys at the garage ______.

e My brother tried to ______ my new slinky.

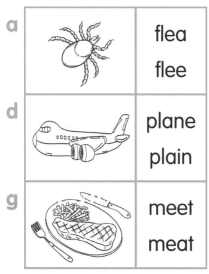

Homophones

1 **Which list word means?**

a a tiny jumping insect with no wings ________

b part of a horse's bridle ________

c a hard strong metal ________

d to run away or escape ________

e an animal that is hunted by another ________

Challenge words

2 **Copy each challenge word.**

wear	________	haul	________
where	________	rays	________
hire	________	raise	________
higher	________	morning	________
hall	________	mourning	________

3 **Color the correct word.**

a I eat breakfast in the [morning] [mourning].

b We enjoyed the warmth of the sun's [raise] [rays].

c We climbed [higher] [hire] up the tree.

d At City [Haul] [Hall] there are lots of old photographs.

e I didn't know [where] [wear] my sister was hiding.

4 **Use as many challenge words as possible to make silly sentences.**

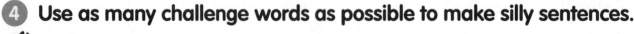

____

____

L.2.2 Demonstrate command of the conventions of standard English capitalization, punctuation, and spelling when writing.

Possessive pronouns

A **pronoun** stands in place of a noun. **Possessive pronouns** show ownership, or possession; e.g., That is **Mason's** bike. That is **his** bike.

1 Circle the correct possessive pronoun.

a The skateboard in the garage is (my, mine).

b The librarian gave us (ours, our) books.

c Amelia is playing with (her, hers) new game.

d Have you made (your, yours) bed yet?

e I asked (mine, my) brother to help me.

f Sarah and Lucy are helping (their, theirs) friends.

2 Complete each sentence with a pronoun from the box.

mine
their his
your her
ours

This is Bella's bag. It is ___her___ bag.

a That is Leo's fish. It is ____________ fish.

b You have two pets. They are ____________ pets.

c The car belongs to me. The car is ____________.

d We have lots of pencils. The pencils are ____________.

e The cards belong to Connor and Declan. They are ____________ cards.

3 Circle the possessive pronouns.

a Where are my keys?

b The dog is in its kennel.

c These books are theirs.

d This hamburger is mine.

A Hairy Question

Visualization

Good readers imagine pictures when they read a text. This is called visualizing. Looking for key words in the text helps you create the images.

Read the passage.

Underline **what** Jan said about cooking.

Circle **what** happened when Jan cooked.

Box **what** Jan said about camping.

Color **what** happened when Jan camped.

The Home Haircut

"Easy," said Jan as she cut. "Piece of cake!"

I remember when Jan said cooking was easy. We spent an afternoon scraping burned food off the stove.

Jan also told me that camping was easy. The tent fell on top of us during the night.

By three o'clock on Saturday afternoon there was more hair on the bathroom floor than on my head.

Circle the correct answer.

1. Which **key word** describes **what** Jan thought about cooking?

   a remember   b scraping   c easy   d more

2. Which phrase helps us **visualize** Jan's cooking?

   a piece of cake   b cooking was easy
   c scraping burned food off the stove   d tent fell on top of us

3. How does this help the reader **see** Jan's cooking adventure? It was ...

   a unsuccessful.   b lots of fun.
   c a great success.   d tasteless.

A Hairy Question

Read the passage.

Circle **what** Jan was doing.

Color words that **describe** Freya's new hairdo.

The Home Haircut

"Look in the mirror, Freya," said Jan.

I did. There was a lot of face and not much hair.

"Is it all right?" Jan said, looking worried.

"One side is longer than the other," I said softly.

Jan cut some more. Snip. Snip. Snip.

In the mirror, I looked strange. My hair was gone. Bits stuck out all over the place.

Jan's face was white.

Underline words that describe **how** Jan **felt**.

1. What does **Freya think** of her new hairdo? ____________________

2. Which **clues** tell you? ____________________

____

3. Draw Freya and Jan's faces in the mirror.

Suffixes: ing, ed

If a verb **ends in a consonant** with a <u>single vowel before it</u>, **double the consonant** before adding the **suffix ing** or **ed**; e.g., ta**p** → ta**pp**ing → ta**pp**ed; gra**b** → gra**bb**ing → gra**bb**ed.

1 **Copy each list word.**

rubbed	rammed	grabbed
jogging	bobbing	stopped
jogged	tipped	trapping
wagging	thinned	blotted
sagged	planned	skinned
sipped	stabbed	flopped
stopping	gripping	

2 **Sort the list words.**

ing	ed
jogging	rubbed

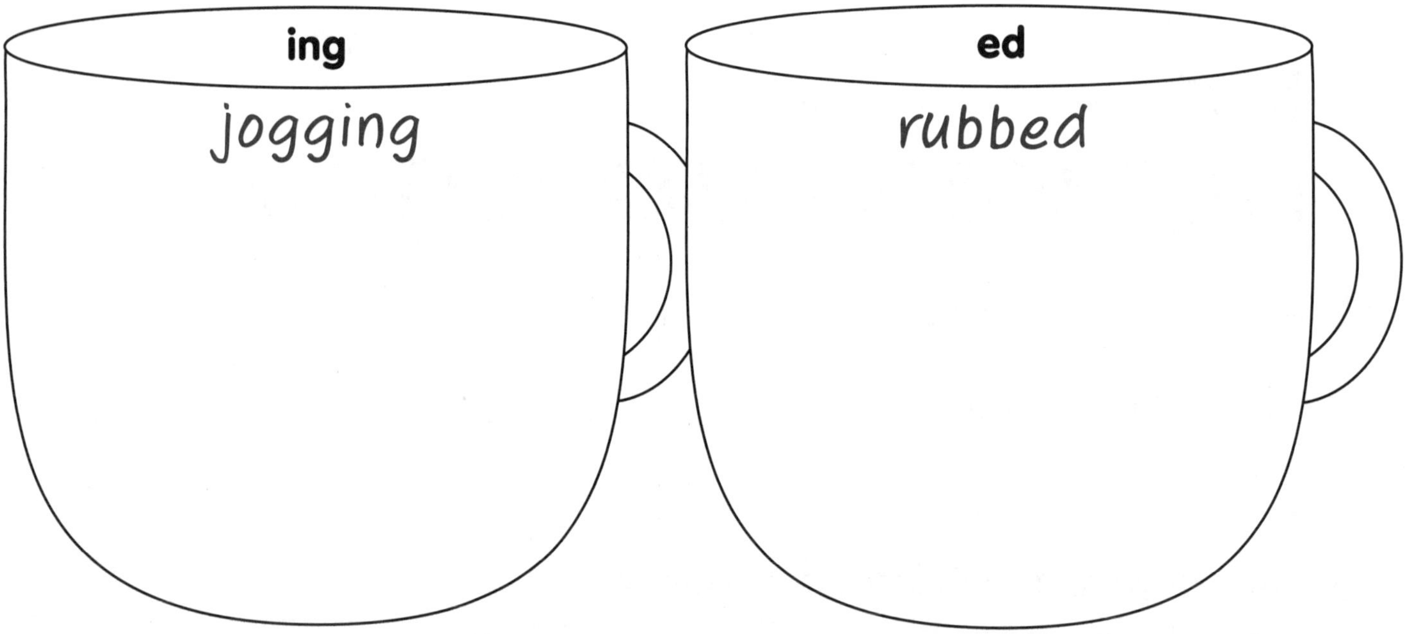

3 **Complete each sentence with a list word.**

a The soccer team is _____ around the oval.

b Yesterday, the soccer team _____ around the oval.

c I _____ the monkey bars tightly so I wouldn't fall.

d The boats are _____ on the water.

L.2.2 Demonstrate command of the conventions of standard English capitalization, punctuation, and spelling when writing.

Suffixes: ing, ed

Challenge words

1 Copy each challenge word.

prodding ______________
stunned ______________
scanning ______________
shipped ______________
knitting ______________
throbbed ______________
strapping ______________
shrugged ______________
scrubbing ______________
squatted ______________

2 Color the correct word.

a We [shiped] [shipped] the package across the country.
b Grandma is [knitting] [kniting] a big woolly sweater.
c My knee [throbbed] [throbed] with pain after I fell over.
d I was [stuned] [stunned] when my painting was chosen.
e She [squatted] [squated] down beside me to take a closer look.

3 Find the hidden challenge word.

a sdjfscanningsggf ______________
b dfsshruggedgvsf ______________
c dgvsscrubbingdfj ______________
d sdfstrappingdfdfs ______________
e ersproddinggfdre ______________

L.2.2 Demonstrate command of the conventions of standard English capitalization, punctuation, and spelling when writing.

Saying verbs

Saying verbs show different ways of saying things; e.g., **whisper, yell, mumble, mutter**. They are a type of **action verb.**

1 Underline the saying verb.

a "What are you doing?" asked Kyle.

b "I'm packing my sleeping bag," replied Sophia.

c "What a huge spider!" exclaimed Sarah.

d "Keep it away from me!" shrieked Ryan.

e "I've hurt my knee," sobbed Erin.

f "I don't know where my keys are," grumbled Grandpa.

g "Watch out!" yelled the man riding behind me.

2 Complete each sentence with a verb from the box.

greeted complained warned cheered
whispered begged gasped

a "You gave me a fright!" ______________ Maria.

b "Hooray! We've won!" ______________ the children.

c "Good morning, Mr. Mendoza," ______________ Joey.

d "Please may I have another slice of pizza," ______________ Ethan.

e "You should take better care of your teeth," ______________ the dentist.

f "Nobody ever listens to me," ______________ Harry.

g "We mustn't let them hear us," ______________ Ella.

L.2.1 Demonstrate command of the conventions of standard English grammar and usage when writing or speaking.

Can I Join the Circus?

Finding the main idea

The main idea of a text is its key point. Details in the text help you find the main idea.

This is part of a script. It is designed to be performed by different people.

Read the passage.

Color **who** is scared.

Underline **why** he is scared.

Box **who** is crying.

Ringmaster Roy: Chuckles, perhaps you could teach Snoz about being a clown.

Narrator: Chuckles had a great time dressing Snoz and painting him with make-up. But when Snoz saw himself in the mirror, he hid under the table.

Snoz: Not funny! Too scary! Snoz is scared!

Narrator: Snoz began to cry. Seeing a Snozalot cry made Chuckles cry too.

Chuckles: (sobbing) That is the saddest thing I have ever seen. A sobbing Snozalot!

Circle the correct answer/s.

1. Find the **main idea** of the text.
   - a Snoz is scared of himself as a clown.
   - b Chuckles is a clown.
   - c Clowns make people laugh.
   - d Snoz can't wait to join the circus.

2. Which two sentences **support** the main idea?
   - a Chuckles had a great time dressing Snoz and painting him with make-up.
   - b But when Snoz saw himself in the mirror, he hid under the table.
   - c Snoz began to cry.
   - d Seeing a Snozalot cry made Chuckles cry too.

Can I Join the Circus?

Read the passage.

Ringmaster Roy: Tell me troupe, what can Snoz the Snozalot Monster do?

Chuckles: I will tell you what he cannot do. He cannot make you laugh.

Bendy Betty: He cannot bend.

Max Manyhands: He cannot juggle.

Ringmaster Roy: I see, I see, I see. And I know he can't fly though the air.

Chuckles: He's a nice monster.

Bendy Betty: A lovely monster, really.

Max Manyhands: But Snoz has no place in Circus Bizurkus.

Circle the things Snoz **cannot** do.

Underline **what** Chuckles says about Snoz.

Box **what** Bendy Betty says about Snoz.

Color **what** Max Manyhands says about Snoz.

1. **Fill in the missing words.**

   The main idea of the text is that ____________ does not belong in ____________.

2. Which **two details** helped you find the main idea?

   a Everyone says Snoz can't ____________

   b Max Manyhands says Snoz has ____________

RL.2.2 Recount stories, including fables and folktales from diverse cultures, and determine their central message, lesson, or moral.

Week 22 Day 3 Spelling

The k sound: k, ck

Two letters that make a single sound are called a **digraph**. The **letters ck** make the **single sound k**. When the **k sound** comes after a single vowel, it is usually **spelled ck**; e.g., fre**ck**le. After a vowel digraph or a consonant, it is **spelled k**; e.g., lea**k**, bas**k**et.

1 Copy each list word.

beak ______	luck ______	mask ______
bank ______	dusk ______	stick ______
lock ______	peck ______	shack ______
tank ______	track ______	stock ______
rock ______	pluck ______	speak ______
pink ______	cheek ______	trunk ______
tick ______	check ______	

2 Write the name for each.

a 

b ______

b 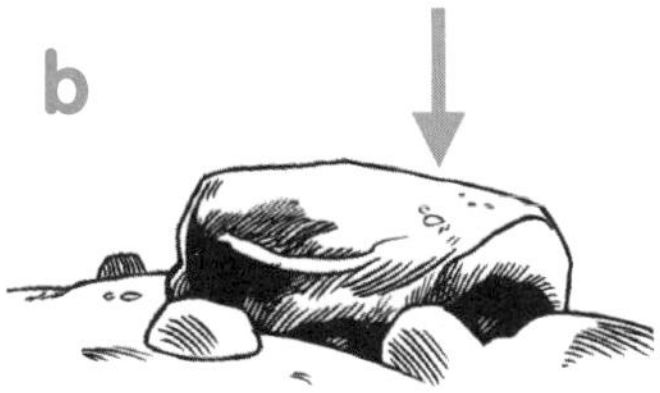

r ______

c 

m ______

d 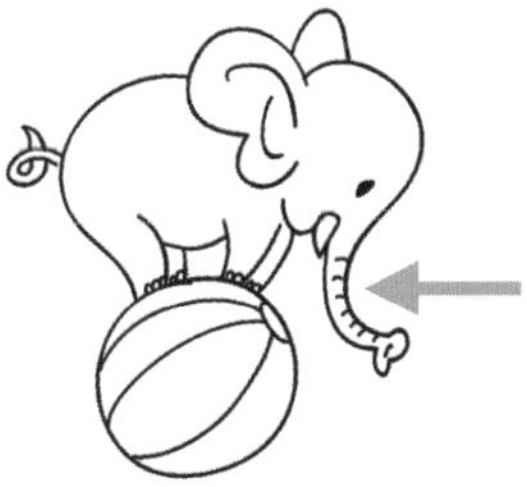

t ______

3 Sort the list words.

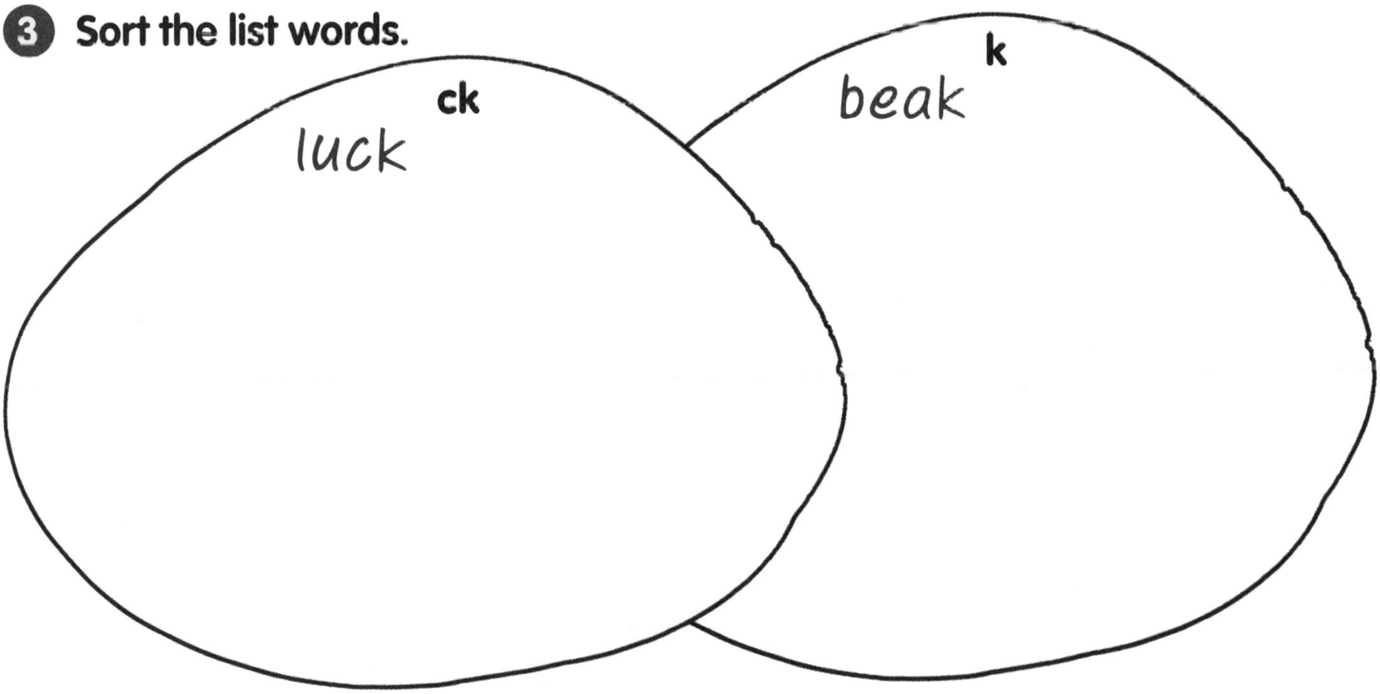

The k sound: k, ck

1 Which list word matches the clue?

a a place you put your money ____________

b the color of a flamingo ____________

c the time of day just before night ____________

Challenge words

2 Copy each challenge word.

soak ____________ stork ____________

cloak ____________ struck ____________

thank ____________ attack ____________

crook ____________ wreck ____________

streak ____________ chipmunk ____________

3 Answer the question with a challenge word.

a What does a superhero wear? ____________

b What bird has very long legs? ____________

c What animal is similar to a squirrel? ____________

d What's another word for thief? ____________

4 Complete each sentence with a challenge word.

a I like to ____________ in a hot bath after a long day.

b I made sure to ____________ her for my birthday present.

c She took off her ____________ and hung it up.

d The ____________ was collecting nuts for the winter.

L.2.2 Demonstrate command of the conventions of standard English capitalization, punctuation, and spelling when writing.

Direct speech

Direct speech repeats the exact words someone says. **Quotation marks (" ")** are placed around the speaker's words, including any punctuation; e.g., "Where are you going?" asked Lola.

1 Underline the speaker's exact words.

a "How many pets have you got?" asked Abigail.

b "I'll wait for you outside," said Owen.

c "How good was that!" exclaimed Lily.

d "Come here at once!" shouted the angry man.

e "I wish I had a pet hamster," sighed the little girl.

f "Now, what have I done with my purse?" mumbled Grandma.

2 Fill in the missing quotation marks.

a How are you feeling today? asked the doctor.

b I would like oatmeal for breakfast, said the child.

c What a large bear! gasped Victoria.

d Don't go too near the edge, warned the ranger.

e I will never do that again, promised Ethan.

3 Write an answer. Don't forget to use quotation marks.

"How old are you, Adam?" asked Sam.

______________________________ said Adam.

The Lion and the Gnat

Finding the main idea

The main idea of a text is its key point. It sums up what the text is about.

Details in the text help you find the main idea.

Read the passage.

Circle the gnat's **actions**.

Underline the lion's **actions**.

Box words that describe the lion's **feelings**.

The gnat dived at the lion and stung him on the nose. The lion was furious! He swiped at the gnat, but only ended up scratching himself with his sharp claws. The gnat attacked the lion again and again, and the lion raged.

Circle the correct answer/s.

1. Which **best** describes the main idea of the text?
   - a A lion attacked a gnat.
   - b A lion fell down.
   - c A gnat wanted to be a lion.
   - d A gnat attacked a lion.

2. Which **two** details **support** the main idea?
   - a The gnat dived at the lion and stung him on the nose.
   - b The lion was furious!
   - c He swiped at the gnat.
   - d The lion scratched himself with his sharp claws.
   - e The gnat attacked the lion again and again, and the lion raged.

3. Which **best** describes the gnat's actions?
   - a selfish
   - b kind
   - c gentle
   - d vicious

RL.2.2 Recount stories, including fables and folktales from diverse cultures, and determine their central message, lesson, or moral.

The Lion and the Gnat

Read the passage.

Underline **what** the lion does.

Color **what** the gnat does.

Finally, the lion was worn out. He was dripping with blood from his own scratches and he lay down, defeated by the gnat. The gnat buzzed away to tell the whole Animal Kingdom about his victory over the lion, but instead he flew straight into a spider's web.

1. What is the **main idea** of the text?
   - a A gnat flew into a spider's web.
   - b The smaller creature proved to be the more dangerous.

2. Which **two details** helped you find the main idea?
   - a The lion was ______________________
   - b The gnat had ______________________

3. What is the **message** from this fable? ______________________

Suffix: ly

Adding the **suffix ly** to an adjective turns it into an adverb; e.g., quick**ly**.
If the adjective ends in y, change the y to i before adding **ly**; e.g., happy → happi**ly**.

1 Copy each list word.

badly ______	mainly ______	largely ______
slowly ______	softly ______	swiftly ______
nicely ______	clearly ______	gently ______
suddenly ______	quickly ______	firmly ______
mostly ______	happily ______	quietly ______
strongly ______	easily ______	fairly ______
shyly ______	calmly ______	

2 Use list words to complete the table.

	bad	badly
a	quick	
b	strong	
c	most	
d	nice	

3 Underline the spelling mistake. Write the word correctly.

a I jumped easly over the short fence. ______

b I quikly ate my dinner so I could play outside. ______

c We spoke sofly so we didn't wake our parents. ______

d I sudenly had a brilliant idea. ______

e The turtle walked slowlee up the beach. ______

L.2.2 Demonstrate command of the conventions of standard English capitalization, punctuation, and spelling when writing.

Suffix: ly

1 Write the list words in alphabetical order.

Challenge words

2 Copy each challenge word.

extremely
actually
finally
slightly
normally
completely
differently
surely
absolutely
equally

3 Color the correct word.

a Mom shared the sushi [eqwually] [equally] between us.

b I [finaly] [finally] finished writing my story.

c We went in [completly] [completely] different directions.

d I am [slightly] [sleightly] taller than my brother.

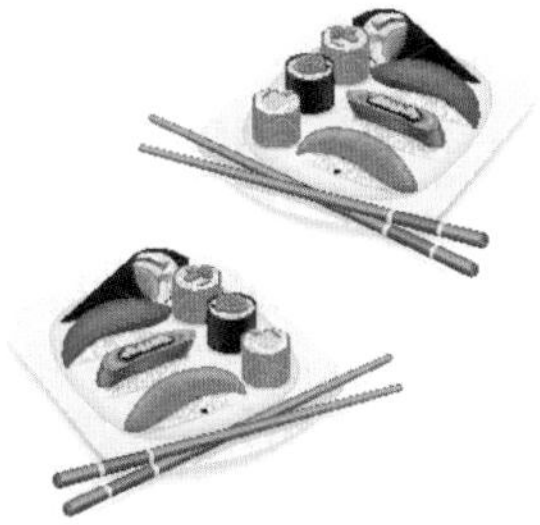

4 Use as many challenge words as possible to make a silly sentence.

Adverbs of manner

Adverbs give information about verbs. **Adverbs of manner** show **how** something is done; e.g., The tortoise moved **slowly** up the beach. Many adverbs of manner end in **ly**.

1 Complete each sentence with an adverb from the box.

a The knight fought ________________.

b The sun is shining ________________.

c We divided the pie ________________.

d The toddler yawned ________________.

e The hungry animals ate ________________.

f ________________, he picked up the tiny kitten.

gently	brightly
sleepily	equally
bravely	greedily

2 Underline the word that is wrong. Write it correctly.

a We shouted loud. ________________

b She eats healthy. ________________

c I fastened my belt loose. ________________

d He painted beautiful. ________________

e She poured the juice careful. ________________

3 Use an adverb to complete the answer.

How did he answer the questions?

He answered the questions ________________.

L.2.1.E Use adverbs.

Dinosaur Dig

Sequencing events
To find the sequence of events in a text, look at numbers and words that give clues to the order in which things happen.

Read the passage.

Circle **where** you might find fossils.

Box **what** the bones are removed from.

Finding Fossils

Places where rocks are eroding might have fossils. Creek banks, dry riverbeds, and cliff faces are all good places to look. Most fossils are covered by a thick layer of rock. At some sites, explosives blow up the rock and bulldozers cart it away. Often the whole block of rock, with its bones, is cut out. This is taken back to the lab where the bones are carefully removed.

1 **Order** what happens when fossils are found.

- ☐ Transport to a lab.
- ☐ Use explosives to blow up the rock.
- ☐ Find dinosaur bones in a rock.
- ☐ Use a bulldozer to remove the rock from the site.
- ☐ In the lab, carefully remove the bones.
- ☐ Find a place with eroding rock—creek bank, riverbed, or cliff face.

2 After this, **where** might children view the fossils? ______________________

Dinosaur Dig

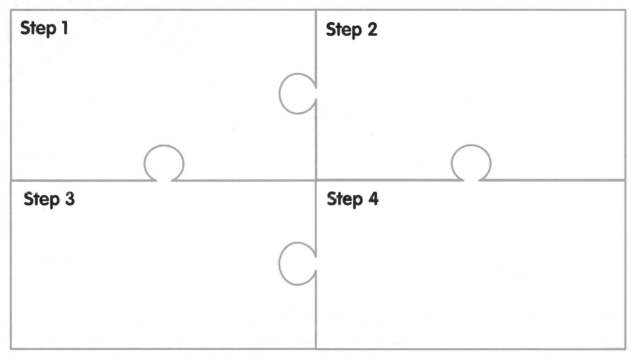

Read the passage.

Giant Jigsaw Puzzles

Putting a dinosaur back together takes skill, patience, and a lot of time.

Using photos and drawings, the skeleton is laid out on the floor and then put back together from the ground up.

Most bones are too fragile to become a skeleton in a museum. A plaster or plastic cast is made. It is rare to find a complete skeleton—most museums' dinosaurs are put together with extra parts.

Underline the **first step** in putting a dinosaur back together.

Color **how** the skeleton is put back together.

Circle **what** happens after photos are taken and drawings made.

1. **Draw** the process of putting together dinosaur skeletons.

Step 1	Step 2
Step 3	Step 4

RI.2.3 Describe the connection between a series of historical events, scientific ideas or concepts, or steps in technical procedures in a text.

Week 24 Day 3 Spelling

Endings: dge, ge

At the end of a word or syllable, the **j sound** is either spelled **dge** or **ge**; e.g., bri**dge**, oran**ge**.

1 Copy each list word.

age		hedge		strange	
edge		fudge		change	
huge		wedge		fringe	
village		bridge		smudge	
badge		image		garage	
large		orange		plunge	
judge		charge			

2 Write the name for each.

a

b ____________

b

o ____________

c
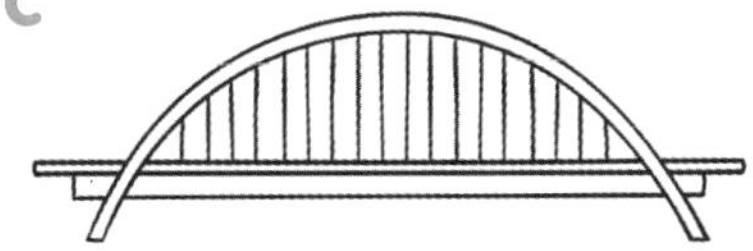
b ____________

d

h ____________

e

j ____________

3 Which list word means?

a a dirty mark or stain ____________

b unusual or odd ____________

c a picture of something ____________

d a round, juicy fruit ____________

e a row of bushes used as a fence ____________

L.2.2 Demonstrate command of the conventions of standard English capitalization, punctuation, and spelling when writing.

Endings: dge, ge

1 Unscramble the letters to make a list word.

a ungple ______

b ngecha ______

c ingefr ______

d agevill ______

e rgecha ______

f raggae ______

Challenge words

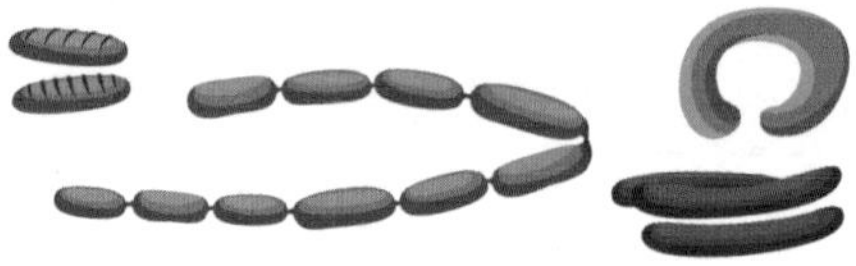

2 Copy each challenge word.

bulge ______

partridge ______

cottage ______

sausage ______

package ______

damage ______

passage ______

manage ______

cringe ______

courage ______

3 Word clues. Which challenge word means?

a a small country house ______

b a wrapped object ______

c the ability to face your fears ______

d a plump bird with brown or gray feathers ______

e can be cooked on a barbecue ______

4 Color the correct word.

a We apologized for the [damage] [damadge] we did to the garden.

b We could see a light at the end of the dark [passadge] [passage].

c I walked to the post office to collect my [package] [packadge].

L.2.2 Demonstrate command of the conventions of standard English capitalization, punctuation, and spelling when writing.

Adverbs of time

Adverbs give information about **verbs**. **Adverbs of time** show **when**, or **how often**, something happens; e.g., We visited our friend **yesterday**.

1 Complete each sentence with an adverb of time.

a I ________________ eat my vegetables.

b I have ________________ seen that movie.

c I hope to finish this book by ________________.

d You can finish your game ________________.

e The comic comes out ________________.

weekly
tomorrow
already
later
always

2 Circle the time adverbs.

a The clock strikes hourly.

b I brush my teeth regularly.

c I have never eaten a snail!

d I saw her in the library earlier.

e The coach wants to see us now.

f I sometimes forget to brush my teeth.

g We're going to watch the ball game tonight.

3 Complete the following sentence.

Yesterday I ____

____

Inventing the Future

Finding facts and information

To find facts and information in a text, ask the questions **Who? What? Where?** or **When?** The answers can be clearly seen in the text.

Read the passage.

A World-changing Gizmo

It all began in 1947. That's when three scientists invented the transistor. The three scientists were from the Bell Laboratories. Their names were John Bardeen, Walter Brattain, and William Shockley.

The first transistor was about the size of your thumb. It was made from a paperclip, gold foil, wire, and a bit of plastic. Transistors were first used in telephones.

Transistors are in computers, the Internet, cell phones, TVs, video cameras, calculators, hand-held games, radar, satellites, and night vision technology.

Circle **who** invented the transistor.

Underline **when** the first transistor was made.

Box **what** the first transistors were made from.

Color **where** transistors were first used.

Circle the correct answer.

1. **What** was the occupation of the inventors?

   a teachers b physiotherapists c scientists d professors

2. **What** size was the first transistor?

   a paperclip-sized b thumb-sized
   c cell phone-sized d telephone-sized

3. **Where** are transistors used today?

   a paperclips b cell phones c plastic d your thumb

RI.2.1 Ask and answer such questions as who, what, where, when, why, and how to demonstrate understanding of key details in a text.

Inventing the Future

Read the passage.

Highlight **what** Dr. Nakamatsu holds the world record for.

Underline **what** Dr. Nakamatsu invented.

Box **when** Dr. Nakamatsu likes inventing.

Color **where** Dr. Nakamatsu invents.

Why Didn't I Think of That?

Dr. Nakamatsu is a modern inventor. He holds the world record for the most patents and inventions. Dr. Nakamatsu has over 3,200 inventions.

Dr. Nakamatsu often came up with ideas underwater. He invented a notepad that he could use underwater to write down his ideas.

Dr. Nakamatsu only sleeps four hours a night. He says the best time for new ideas is between midnight and 4 a.m. He has two special rooms that help him think.

1. **What** was Dr. Nakamatsu's underwater problem?

____

2. **What** was Dr. Nakamatsu's solution?

____

3. Think of a problem that you could invent a gizmo for.

Who would need it?	**What** would it be?	**Where** would it be used?	**When** would it be needed?

Compound words

Compound words are formed when two or more words join together to make a new word; e.g., hairbrush.

1 Copy each list word.

armpit ______	windmill ______	eyebrow ______
pancake ______	raincoat ______	handshake ______
freeway ______	snowman ______	rainfall ______
starfish ______	backpack ______	leftovers ______
shoelace ______	grandchild ______	teardrop ______
anybody ______	hairbrush ______	strawberry ______
uphill ______	driveway ______	

2 Add the pictures to make a list word.

a  +  = ______

b  +  = ______

c  +  = ______

d  + 

= ______

L.2.2 Demonstrate command of the conventions of standard English capitalization, punctuation, and spelling when writing.

Compound words

1 Underline the spelling mistake. Write the word correctly.

a Strawbery is my favorite flavor of ice cream. ____________

b In winter we like to go outside and build a snoman. ____________

c On rainy days I pack my umbrella and raincote. ____________

d I packed my hat and sunscreen into my bakpack. ____________

e I couldn't find my harebrush so I had to use my comb. ____________

Challenge words

2 Copy each challenge word.

outdoors	____________	background	____________
marketplace	____________	doughnut	____________
elsewhere	____________	clockwork	____________
downstairs	____________	earphone	____________
watermelon	____________	cheeseburger	____________

3 Complete each sentence with a challenge word.

a When I eat ____________ I always spit out the black seeds.

b Dad told us to go and play ____________.

c We brought home a huge box of peaches from the ____________.

d I wanted the ____________ with pink frosting and sprinkles.

4 Which challenge word means?

a a large round fruit with green skin ____________

b to run smoothly ____________

Noun phrases

A **phrase** is a part of a sentence. It does not make sense on its own. A **noun phrase** is a group of words built around a noun. It can include **articles**, (a, an, the), **pronouns** (my, his, her), and **adjectives** (small, new, red); e.g., a pepperoni pizza, his silver helmet.

1 Circle the noun in each phrase.

a a new barbecue

b my red umbrella

c the sweet candy

d an old man

e their big pickup

f two little mice

g a rainy day

h a blue bat

i an oval shape

2 Complete each sentence with an adjective from the box.

tiny electric fluffy dirty new juicy

a My friend has a ________________ white cat.

b He is eating a soft, ________________ peach.

c His boat has an ________________ motor.

d I watched the ________________ ant crawl up the wall.

e My friend let me ride his ________________ sled.

f She removed the ________________ mark from her shirt.

Boats

Compare and contrast

Compare and contrast information by looking for the **similarities** and **differences**.

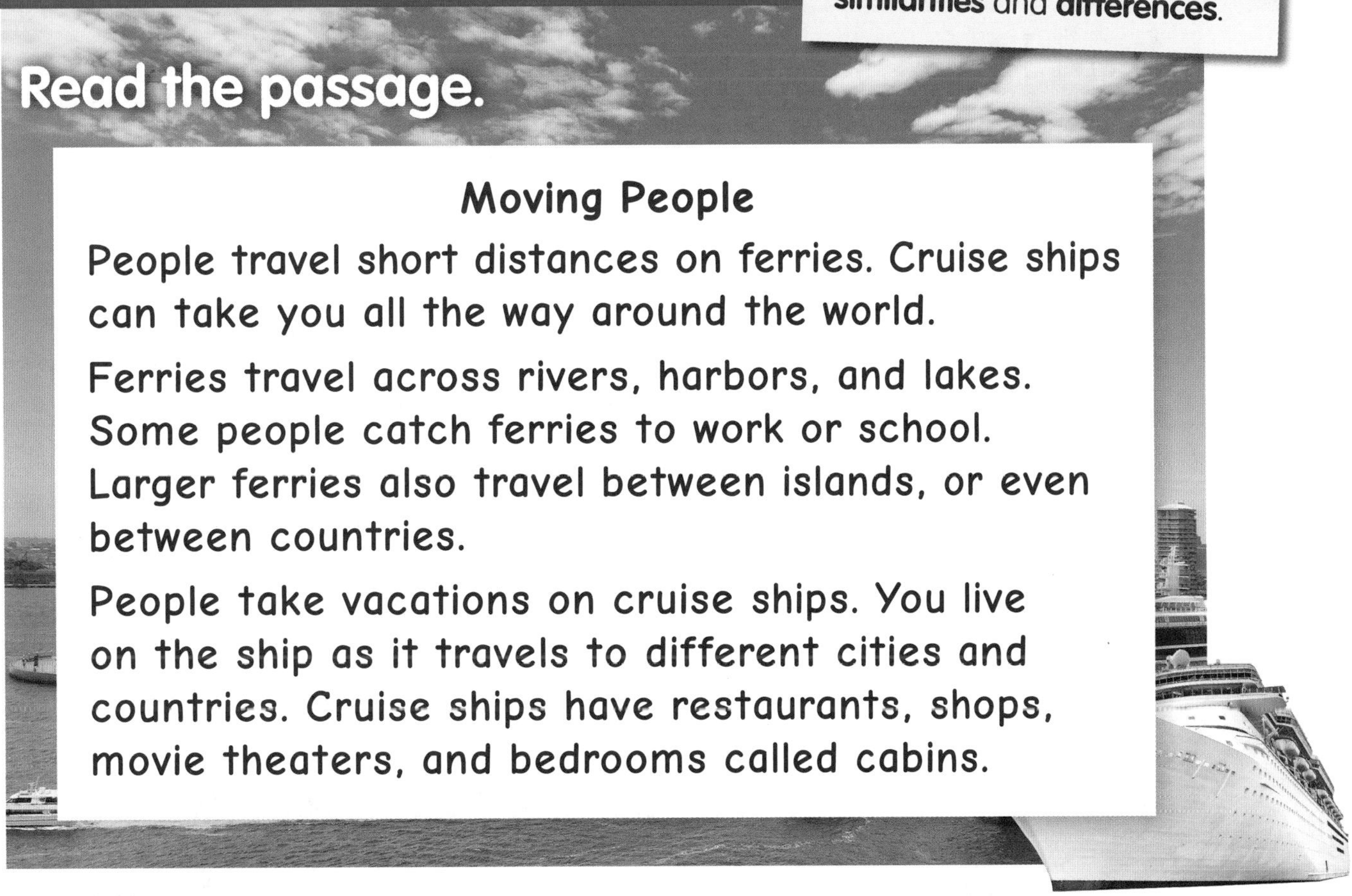

Read the passage.

Moving People

People travel short distances on ferries. Cruise ships can take you all the way around the world.

Ferries travel across rivers, harbors, and lakes. Some people catch ferries to work or school. Larger ferries also travel between islands, or even between countries.

People take vacations on cruise ships. You live on the ship as it travels to different cities and countries. Cruise ships have restaurants, shops, movie theaters, and bedrooms called cabins.

1. Compare and contrast everyday boats we use. Tick [✔] the correct answers on the table.

	Travels on and between					Travel for			Time spent on board		On board		
	rivers	harbors	lakes	cities	countries	work	holiday	school	minutes or hours	days or weeks	shops	movie theaters	restrooms
ferry													
cruise ship													

Use the information in the table to answer the questions below.

2. What would you find on **both** ferries and cruise ships?

____

3. Between which two places do both ferries and cruise ships travel?

____

Boats

Read the passage.

The Navy

Destroyers, submarines, and aircraft carriers are all used by the navy.

Destroyers are fast. They are often used to protect bigger, slower ships. They can hold up to 300 people.

Submarines travel under the water. They hold up to 150 people and can move quickly if they must.

Aircraft carriers are the biggest ships in the navy. They carry planes which can take off and land on their long decks. They can have up to 5,000 sailors and pilots on board at any one time.

1 Complete the table.

Boat	What does it do?	How many people can it hold?	Interesting fact
destroyer			
submarine			
aircraft carrier			

2 **How** are destroyers, submarines, and aircraft carriers similar?

____

RI.2.1 Ask and answer such questions as who, what, where, when, why, and how to demonstrate understanding of key details in a text.

Contractions

A **contraction** is two words joined to make a shorter word. The left out letters are replaced by an **apostrophe** ('); e.g., you will → you'll.

1 Copy each list word.

I'm	______	we'll	______	hasn't	______
he's	______	don't	______	where's	______
it's	______	she'll	______	what's	______
I've	______	it'd	______	you'd	______
how's	______	who's	______	can't	______
there's	______	it'll	______	didn't	______
won't	______	who'll	______		

2 Underline the spelling mistake. Write the word correctly.

a Jay told me that h'es not coming to the party. ______

b I cant' stand on my head! ______

c Don't worry, she'l be here any minute. ______

d Im the tallest player in my basketball team. ______

e I'ts been two weeks since I've seen my friend. ______

3 Draw a line to match the words to their contractions.

has not	didn't
a where is	hasn't
b did not	how's
c I have	where's
d how is	I've

Contractions

1 Rewrite the contraction correctly.

a itll ______________ b well ______________

c wont ______________ d youd ______________

Challenge words

2 Copy each challenge word.

wasn't	______	haven't	______
they've	______	doesn't	______
you're	______	o'clock	______
mustn't	______	couldn't	______
weren't	______	would've	______

3 Which list word means?

a were not ______________ b would have ______________

c does not ______________ d was not ______________

e could not ______________ f you are ______________

4 Color the correct word.

a I [wasn't] [wan'st] sure which direction we should take.

b You [musun't] [mustn't] make a sound or you'll wake the baby.

c I [couldn't] [could't] go to football practice because I'd lost my boots.

d The hike starts promptly at nine [o'clock] [oclock].

L.2.2 Demonstrate command of the conventions of standard English capitalization, punctuation, and spelling when writing.

Adjectives and adverbs

Adjectives give information about nouns and pronouns; e.g., He is a **tall** boy. He is **tall**. **Adverbs** give information about verbs; e.g., They ski **quickly**.

1 Circle the adjective that gives information about the noun.

a There were six **eggs** in the nest.

b Yesterday I rode my new **skateboard** to the park.

c The hungry **caterpillar** ate everything in sight.

d They were sitting in the front **row** of the theater.

e We saw models of huge **dinosaurs** at the museum.

2 Circle the adverb that gives information about the verb.

a The girl **spoke** clearly into the microphone.

b The marshmallows **roasted** quickly over the hot fire.

c I carefully **placed** the glass on the shelf.

d The child **greeted** the mayor politely.

3 Circle the adjective and underline the adverb.

a The young choir sang beautifully.

b The large lion roared fiercely.

c The little star shone brightly.

Mammals

Making inferences

Use **clues** in the text to make an inference.

The clues help you find the answers that are hiding in the text.

Read the passage.

Hoofed Mammals

Hoofed mammals eat plants. They are herbivores. Zebras, giraffes, and elephants are all hoofed mammals.

Many hoofed mammals live in groups called herds. They often live on open plains or grasslands. The herd moves from place to place in search of food. Zebras and wildebeests live in large herds.

Elephants are the largest land animals. They live in family groups called herds. Baby elephants feed on mother's milk for two years while they grow.

Circle the **hoofed animals**.

Underline the **collective noun**.

Box **two verbs** that tell what baby elephants do.

Circle the correct answer.

1. Which **best** describes how hoofed animals live?
   - a in harmony with many other animals
   - b on their own
   - c in pairs
   - d in large groups

2. Which **clue** tells you this?
   - a Hoofed mammals eat plants.
   - b Zebras, giraffes, and elephants are all hoofed mammals.
   - c Many hoofed mammals live in groups called herds.
   - d The herd moves from place to place in search of food.
   - e Elephants are the largest land animals.

RI.2.1 Ask and answer such questions as who, what, where, when, why, and how to demonstrate understanding of key details in a text.

Mammals

Read the passage.

Underline the word that **compares** the **size** of apes and monkeys.

Box the word that **compares** the **size** of gorillas and other apes.

Monkeys and Apes

Monkeys and apes are mammals called primates. They are warm-blooded, furry animals that suckle their young.

Baboons, mandrills, and howlers are all monkeys. Monkeys are very good climbers. They use their hands, feet, and tails to help them climb.

Apes are larger than monkeys. Chimpanzees, gibbons, orangutans, and gorillas are all apes. Apes do not have tails.

Gorillas are the largest of all the apes and are tailless. They live in family groups.

Color **which** primates have tails.

Circle **which** primates don't have tails.

1 Use the information to order the size of primates.

small	larger	largest

2 What is the physical difference between monkeys and apes?

____

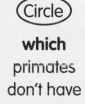

3 Which **clue** tells you? ______________________

____

RI.2.1 Ask and answer such questions as who, what, where, when, why, and how to demonstrate understanding of key details in a text.

Week 27 Day 3 Spelling

Plurals: s, es

We can change nouns from singular to plural nouns by adding the **suffix s** or **es**; e.g., spider**s**, kiss**es**.

1 Copy each list word.

pigs		cages		classes	
bees		eyes		flashes	
foxes		lions		bunches	
dishes		tricks		kisses	
books		things		sharks	
rocks		plants		lambs	
coats		spiders			

2 Write the singular and plural for each word.

a				
b				
c	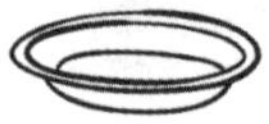			
d				
e				
f	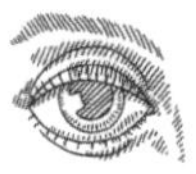			
g				
h				

L.2.2 Demonstrate command of the conventions of standard English capitalization, punctuation, and spelling when writing.

Plurals: s, es

1 Complete each sentence with a list word.

a There were two ______________ rolling in the mud.

b We could hear the ______________ roaring loudly from their cave.

c I watched several ______________ buzzing noisily around the garden.

d I hung all the ______________ in the closet.

e I borrowed two new ______________ from the library.

f The florist had ______________ of beautiful flowers outside her shop.

Challenge words

2 Copy each challenge word.

fingers	______________	branches	______________
flowers	______________	quizzes	______________
monkeys	______________	oranges	______________
catches	______________	giraffes	______________
watches	______________	cabbages	______________

3 Answer the question with a challenge word.

a What kinds of animals have long necks? ______________

b What do bees collect pollen from? ______________

c What do you have on your hands? ______________

d What kind of fruit grows on trees? ______________

4 Complete each sentence with a challenge word.

a The ______________ sat in the tree eating bananas.

b I have five ______________ on one hand and five toes on one foot.

Contractions

A **contraction** is a shorter way of writing a word or words. To make the contraction, letters are left out. An **apostrophe (')** shows where the letters have been left out; e.g., **I will** help you. **I'll** help you.

1 Replace the underlined words with a contraction.

a She has not found her hockey stick. ______

b I cannot solve this problem. ______

c I have finished the pumpkin pie. ______

d That is not my sweater. ______

e They are not at home. ______

I've
hasn't
aren't
can't
isn't

2 Which letters does the apostrophe replace?

we will	we'll	wi
a she is	she's	______
b they are	they're	______
c do not	don't	______
d you have	you've	______

3 Write the words correctly.

mustve	must've	a theyll	______
b didnt	______	c thats	______
d havent	______	e doesnt	______

L.2.2.C Use an apostrophe to form contractions.

Spelling

Use this review to test your knowledge. It has three parts—**Spelling**, **Grammar**, and **Comprehension**. If you're unsure of an answer, go back and read the rules and generalizations in the blue boxes.

You have learned about:

- suffixes: er, est
- the k sound: k, ck
- compound words
- homophones
- suffix: ly
- contractions
- suffixes: ing, ed
- endings: dge, ge
- plurals: s, es

1 Complete. 2 marks

a one spider, but two ______________

b one branch, but two ______________

2 Which word completes the sentence? 1 mark

It was the ______________ winter in thirty years.

a colder b cold c coldest d colds

3 Color the letter/s that correctly completes each word. 1 mark

a chee | ck | k | b bri | dge | ge |

4 Complete the contractions. 2 marks

a who is → ______________ b would have → ______________

5 Which word completes the sentence? 1 mark

Our family finished the ______________ pie.

a whole b hole c holey d wholes

6 Name the compound word. 1 mark

 +  = ______________

7 Which word completes the sentence? 1 mark

My pony ______________ jumped the fence.

a easy b easily c easier d easiest

8 Underline the spelling mistake. Spell it correctly. 1 mark

I am kniting a scarf. ______________

Your score ☐ / 10

Grammar

You have learned about:

- possessive nouns
- direct speech
- noun phrases
- possessive pronouns
- adverbs of manner
- adjectives and adverbs
- saying verbs
- adverbs of time
- contractions

1 Add the apostrophes. 2 marks

a That is Dans book.

b The babys toy is in the box.

2 Circle the correct possessive pronoun. 2 marks

a The bat is (her, hers), not (your, yours).

b (Their, Theirs) pencils are on the table, and (my, mine) are in the drawer.

3 Complete each sentence with a verb from the box. 2 marks

whispered	yelled

a Rosie ______________________ at the top of her voice.

b Sid ______________________ a secret in my ear.

4 Add in the missing quotation marks. 2 marks

a How many candies have you had? asked Joey.

b Not half as many as you, replied Ella.

Grammar

5 Underline the word that is wrong. Write it correctly. 4 marks

a They spoke soft. ______________

b She tied it tight. ______________

c He walked quick. ______________

d It is raining heavy. ______________

6 Color the time adverbs. 2 marks

a They will be here later.

b Come here immediately!

7 Underline the noun in each phrase. 2 marks

a two furry little squirrels

b a long wooden table

8 Color the adjective and underline the adverb. 2 marks

a The little calf ran quickly to its mother.

b The orange leaves floated gently to the ground.

9 Write the contractions of the underlined words. 2 marks

a <u>We will</u> help you if we can. ______________

b <u>It is</u> your turn next. ______________

Your score ___ / 20

Ming Ming's Adventure

Read the passage and then answer the questions.

Ming Ming lived in the village of Jizhou. She was a daydreamer. She liked to pretend she was a princess.

Her father complained that she was a lazy child, but her mother said she had a good heart.

One day, Ming Ming's mother sent Ming Ming into the mountains to collect herbs. Her mother warned her to concentrate because the paths were dangerous.

Ming Ming set off. Before long, she was lost in her own imaginary world and tripped over a fallen log. She fell and smashed the special basket her mother had given her.

"Oh no!" she cried. "How will I carry the herbs home? Mother will never forgive me."

As Ming Ming wiped away her tears, she noticed some hollow seed pods nearby. She would use those to carry the herbs she collected.

When Ming Ming returned to the village, she told her parents what had happened. Her father praised his daughter for clever thinking.

1. Which country is the village of Jizhou likely to be in? 1 mark — INFERENTIAL

   a Australia b America c England d China

2. We can infer that Ming Ming didn't always do her chores. Which phrase is the clue? 1 mark — INFERENTIAL

   a a good heart b a lazy child c a quiet spot d a young girl

Ming Ming's Adventure

3 Why did Ming Ming go into the mountains? 1 mark — LITERAL

a to pick flowers
b to collect herbs
c to sit and daydream
d to look for seed pods

4 Which words best describe Ming Ming? 1 mark — CRITICAL

a lazy and cruel
b kind and imaginative
c hardworking and clever
d clumsy and sad

5 Which word is closest in meaning to *concentrate*? 1 mark — VOCABULARY

a listen
b watch
c focus
d manage

6 What happened first? 1 mark — LITERAL

a Ming Ming collected the herbs.
b The basket broke.
c Ming Ming tripped.
d Ming Ming saw the seed pods.

7 Why was Ming Ming crying? She ... 1 mark — INFERENTIAL

a was upset about the broken basket.
b hurt herself when she tripped.
c was scared of her father.
d couldn't find any herbs.

8 What is the main purpose of the text? 1 mark — CRITICAL

a to give information
b to tell a story
c to explain how something works
d to state a point of view

9 What is the main message of the text? 1 mark — LITERAL

a Respect your parents.
b Take care of other people's things.
c Every problem has a solution.
d Look where you're going.

Your score ☐ / 10

10 Why did Ming Ming's father praise his daughter? For her ... 1 mark — LITERAL

a honesty
b cleverness
c bravery
d hard work

Your Review 3 Scores

Spelling		Grammar		Comprehension		Total
☐	+	☐	+	☐	=	☐
10		20		10		40

Computer Virus

Drawing conclusions

To draw conclusions from a text, use clues to make your own judgments.

The clues help you find the answers that are hiding in the text.

Read the passage.

Circle three verbs that show **how Vinnie moved**.

Underline Vinnie's **dialogue**.

Box a word that shows **how Vinnie's mom felt**.

Color Mom's **dialogue**.

The Sniffles

Vinnie raced in the front door. His bag skidded across the living room floor.

"What's going on in here?" Vinnie's mom stood in the doorway, hands on her hips.

Vinnie walked over and picked up his bag.

"Sorry, Mom. I'm in a bit of a hurry."

"What about a snack?"

"I'm not hungry."

Mary stood in shock as she watched him run up the stairs.

Circle the correct answer/s.

1 Which is the best **conclusion**?

a Vinnie was in a rush.
b Vinnie likes doing his homework.
c Vinnie is hungry.
d Vinnie likes to keep things neat and tidy.

2 Which two words are **clues** to question 1's answer?

a walked
b raced
c run
d stood

3 Which is the best **conclusion**?

a Mom is untidy and doesn't like tidying.
b Mom doesn't like making snacks.
c Mom was surprised Vinny didn't want a snack.
d Vinnie was tired from a long day at school.

Computer Virus

Read the passage.

Color words that describe **Dr. Hacker's arrival**.

Box Dr. Hacker's **dialogue**.

Dr. Hacker

Vinnie pulled the ad from his pocket and dialled the number.

"Hello," said the voice on the other end of the line.

"Are you Dr. Hacker?" asked Vinnie.

"That's right."

Vinnie explained his problem.

"Never fear, young Vinnie. I'll be there in a flash," said Dr. Hacker.

Vinnie hung up. Smoke filled the hall and a flash of light blinded him.

Dr. Hacker waved away the smoke. "Show me your sick computer."

Underline Vinnie's **dialogue**.

1. What can we **conclude** about Vinnie's problem?

   ____

2. From his arrival, what can we **conclude** about Dr. Hacker?

   ____

3. Which **clues** tell you?

   The text says, " ______________________________

   ____

Irregular past tense verbs

Irregular verbs do not use the **suffix ed** in the past tense. Some irregular verbs change their spelling and sound different in the past tense; e.g., I **eat** my apple. I **ate** my apple.

1 Copy each list word.

did	______	awoke	______	forgot	______
ate	______	became	______	froze	______
fled	______	began	______	swung	______
gave	______	bound	______	flung	______
went	______	clung	______	fought	______
stole	______	sprang	______	chose	______
shook	______	knew	______		

2 Unscramble these list words.

a mecabe ______ b undbo ______

c ngaspr ______ d ghtfou ______

e ungsw ______ f okeaw ______

3 Complete the list words.

a d__d b cl__ __g c ch__ __e d fr__z__ e s__ __l__

4 Underline the spelling mistake. Write the word correctly.

a I awake in the middle of the night. ______

b After his bath, the dog shake water everywhere. ______

c Yesterday I eat five sandwiches and two granola bars. ______

d Mom give me some money to buy bread. ______

e I forget to pack my overdue library books. ______

L.2.2 Demonstrate command of the conventions of standard English capitalization, punctuation, and spelling when writing.

Irregular past tense verbs

Challenge words

1 Copy each challenge word.

built	______	caught	______
brought	______	dealt	______
taught	______	heard	______
struck	______	meant	______
shrank	______	understood	______

2 Color the correct word.

a I [bring] [brought] chocolate fudge brownies to the picnic.

b I [taught] [teach] my little sister how to count to five.

c The branch [struck] [strike] me in the back of the head.

d I hope she [understood] [understand] my instructions.

e I [caught] [catch] the ball before it hit the window.

3 Which challenge word means?

a past tense of catch ______

b past tense of shrink ______

c past tense of bring ______

d past tense of strike ______

e past tense of teach ______

f past tense of build ______

Irregular past tense verbs

Past tense verbs show that an action has already happened. Some past tense verbs are formed by adding **ed** to the present form; e.g., They talk**ed**.

Irregular verbs change in other ways, or do not change at all; e.g., break → broke, read → read.

1 Draw lines to match the verbs.

Present tense	Past tense
grow	went
a think	felt
b buy	brought
c fall	thought
d bring	grew
e go	bought
f feel	fell

2 Write the following verbs in the past tense.

a give ______

b eat ______

c is ______

d win ______

e steal ______

f begin ______

g has ______

3 Write the words in the past tense to complete each sentence.

a I (know) ______ the answer.

b We (tell) ______ them what to do.

c They (sit) ______ on the bench.

d She (writes) ______ in her book.

e The bird (flies) ______ away.

f I (see) ______ a rhino at the zoo.

g He (makes) ______ a paper hat.

h She (teaches) ______ me to read.

L.2.1.D Form and use the past tense of frequently occurring irregular verbs.

Game Plan

Making predictions

You can predict what is going to happen in a text based on clues in the words and pictures.

Read the passage.

Dear Sophie,

Thanks for your letter. I am sending you and your friend Luke my latest Cosmic Creature called Radiant. I would be delighted to share a few tricks of the trade with you and Luke. I will send my helicopter to pick you up at 10:15 a.m. this Saturday, from the soccer field near your house. Bring Gizmo along too.

Don't be late. I don't like to wait.

Yours in fun,
Professor Flukelar

Circle the correct answers.

1. Which **two predictions** can you make about what will happen in the story?
   - a Luke will forget to bring Gizmo, and Professor Flukelar will be angry.
   - b Sophie and Luke will spend the day with Professor Flukelar.
   - c Sophie will break her Cosmic Creature because she doesn't like it.
   - d Sophie and Luke will learn many new ideas from Professor Flukelar.

2. What **evidence** is there in the text to support your predictions?
   - a Don't be late.
   - b I am sending you and your friend Luke my latest Cosmic Creature called Radiant.
   - c I would be delighted to share a few tricks of the trade with you and Luke.
   - d Thanks for your letter.
   - e Bring Gizmo along too.

Game Plan

Read the passage.

'What if ...'

"But how do you think of things like that?" asked Sophie.

"Yeah," said Luke. "How do you get to be the one who sees something in a new way, when no one else has?"

"Well," said the professor, smiling, "there are a few little tricks that I can share with you."

The professor led them into his workroom. It was lined with his wonderful creations. All the Cosmic Creatures were there, as well as his siren balls, superfast glider kits, and stretchable blocks.

1. **What** will Sophie and Luke learn from Professor Flukelar?

   ____

2. Predict **one** piece of advice the professor will give Sophie and Luke.

   ____

3. Draw what a Cosmic Creature might look like.

 RL.2.7 Use information gained from the illustrations and words in a print or digital text to demonstrate understanding of its characters, setting, or plot.

Split digraphs

Two letters that make a single sound are called a **digraph**. When **vowel digraphs** are separated by a consonant, they become **split digraphs**; e.g., ba**k**e, bo**n**e, ru**l**e.

1 Copy each list word.

face	______	stone	______	prune	______
safe	______	smile	______	slide	______
nine	______	rule	______	skate	______
bone	______	alone	______	blade	______
June	______	stole	______	shade	______
these	______	glide	______	whole	______
close	______	plate	______		

2 Write the name for each.

a 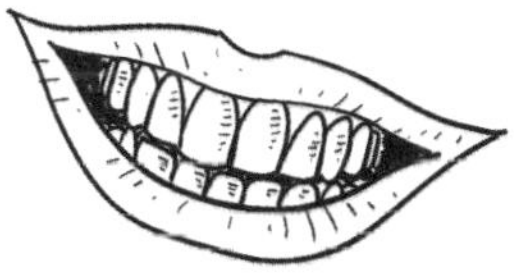
s ______

b 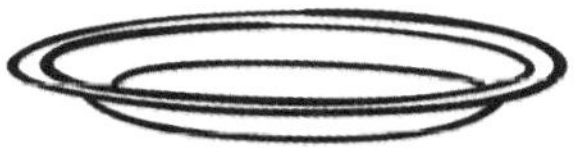
p ______

c 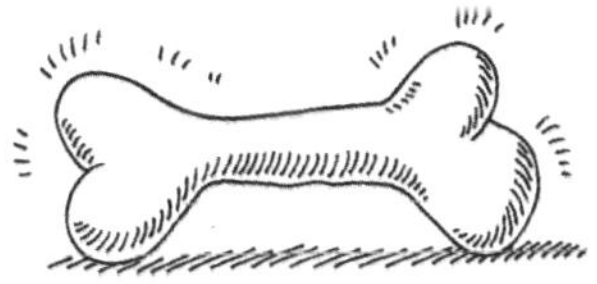
b ______

d 
n ______

3 Write the list word that belongs in each group.

a skeleton, skin, ______

b grin, laugh, ______

c bowl, cup, ______

d rock, pebble, ______

e knife, sword, ______

f seven, eight, ______

4 Sort each list word into a column.

a-e	e-e	i-e	o-e	u-e

Split digraphs

Challenge words

1 Copy each challenge word.

scrape	______	guide	______
while	______	lemonade	______
shave	______	microwave	______
tadpole	______	crocodile	______
gnome	______		
whale	______		

2 Answer the question with a challenge word.

a What reptile has large snapping jaws with lots of sharp teeth? ______

b What delicious drink can you make with lemons, sugar, and water? ______

c What is a young frog called? ______

d What animal lives underwater and blows water through its blowhole? ______

e What do you use to heat up food? ______

3 Complete each sentence with a challenge word.

a I had to ______ the melted cheese off the pan.

b Dad uses a razor and soap to ______ his face.

c The ______ had started to grow long legs.

d Grandma bought a new ______ for her garden.

L.2.2 Demonstrate command of the conventions of standard English capitalization, punctuation, and spelling when writing.

Prepositions

Prepositions are important words that come before **nouns** and **pronouns**. They help to tell **where**, **when**, or **how**; e.g., **in** the house, **at** midday, **with** a spoon.

1 Circle the correct preposition.

a We are going (to, for) the library.

b He looked (on, out) the window.

c They walked (past, up) the museum.

d I sat (from, beside) my friend on the bus.

e I cleaned it (above, with) soap and water.

f I bought my mother a box (to, of) candy.

g I heard a scream (on, in) the middle of the night.

2 Complete each sentence with a preposition from the box. Use each preposition once.

past	on
above	at
for	in
under	

a I waited ____________ the train station.

b We drove ____________ an amusement park.

c The clouds float ____________ the earth.

d My friend's party is ____________ Saturday.

e My cat was hiding ____________ my bed.

f We haven't seen them ____________ a long time.

g She blew out the candles ____________ a single breath.

3 Use the picture to help you complete the sentences.

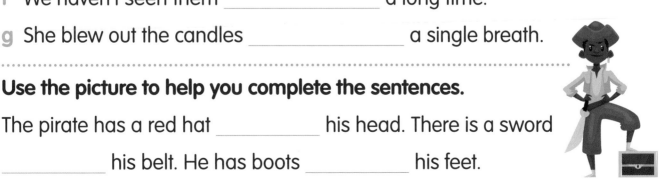

The pirate has a red hat __________ his head. There is a sword __________ his belt. He has boots __________ his feet.

L.2.1 Demonstrate command of the conventions of standard English grammar and usage when writing or speaking.

Haikus

Visualization

Good readers imagine pictures when they read. They use their senses to help them visualize.

Haiku poems show a moment in time. They have few words and readers fill in the gaps by visualizing.

Read the passage.

Circle **what** is in the room.

Box the **punctuation marks**.

A man, just one—
also a fly, just one—
in the huge drawing room

Kobayashi Issa

Underline the **adjectives**.

Color the **repeated** phrase.

Circle the correct answers.

1. Which **two** things are in the drawing room?

   a man b huge c bay d fly

2. Which **two** punctuation marks are used?

   a question marks b commas
   c colons d dashes

3. **What** do these punctuation marks tell the reader to do?

   a shout b pause c whisper d look up

4. Which word **best** describes how the drawing room would look?

   a crowded b empty c full d noisy

RL.2.4 Describe how words and phrases (e.g., regular beats, alliteration, rhymes, repeated lines) supply rhythm and meaning in a story, poem, or song.

Haikus

Read the passage.

Circle the **sound** words.

Box the word that describes the **feel** of the egg.

Warm snug speckled egg
Dappled light fading quickly
Soft crack of split shell

Alysha Hodge

Underline words that describe what the egg **looks like**.

Color words that describe the **light**.

Circle the correct answer.

1. At what **time of day** is the poet looking at the egg?
   a morning b late at night c midday d late afternoon

2. Which phrase describes the **sound** of the egg breaking?
   a dappled b warm snug c fading quickly d soft crack

3. To hear this sound, how far away is the poet from the egg?
   a far away b behind it in a field
   c very close d in the next town

4. What is the poet **seeing**?
   a a person taking a photo of an egg
   b two chickens wrapped in a warm blanket
   c two farmers ploughing the field
   d a bird hatching

Digraphs: ea, ee

Two letters that make a single sound are called a **digraph**. The **letters ea** make the **single sound ee**; e.g., **tea**m. The **letters ee** also make the **single sound ee**; e.g., tr**ee**. When the **digraph ee** is **separated by a consonant**, it becomes a **split digraph**; e.g., th**e**s**e**.

1 Copy each list word.

meet ______	beat ______	pleat ______
meat ______	sheet ______	wheat ______
feet ______	neat ______	bleat ______
heat ______	treat ______	upbeat ______
greet ______	sweet ______	street ______
seat ______	cheat ______	repeat ______
fleet ______	tweet ______	

2 Sort the list words.

3 Complete each sentence with a list word.

a I opened the door to ______ our visitors.

b In summer I only need a light ______ on my bed.

c I couldn't find my shoes, so I ran to the shops in bare ______.

d My friend and I live on the same ______.

L.2.2 Demonstrate command of the conventions of standard English capitalization, punctuation, and spelling when writing.

Digraphs: ea, ee

1 Which list word means?

a a group of ships ______

b the sound made by a goat or sheep ______

c to win against another ______

d the sound made by a bird ______

e grain from certain grasses ______

Challenge words

2 Copy each challenge word.

compete ______

delete ______

defeat ______

overeat ______

athlete ______

parakeet ______

retreat ______

complete ______

concrete ______

heartbeat ______

3 Which challenge word means?

a to eat too much ______

b to move back or away from something ______

c someone who participates in sports ______

d a small, brightly colored bird ______

4 Color the correct word.

a I decided not to [compete] [compet] in this year's fun run.

b I ran a [complet] [complete] circuit of the sports field.

c The doctor used a stethoscope to listen to my [heartbeat] [heartbeet].

Adverbial phrases

A **phrase** is a group of words that does not make complete sense. Many phrases that start with a **preposition** do the work of an adverb. They tell us **where, when**, or **how**; e.g., **in** the ocean, **at** midnight, **with** a smile.

1 Complete each sentence with a preposition from the box.

a The boy was leaning __________ the wall.

b The pie is baking __________ the oven.

c I haven't eaten __________ this morning.

d She washed her hands __________ special soap.

since
in
against
with

2 Does the underlined phrase tell where, when, or how?

a The party starts **at two o'clock**. __________

b The baby dropped the spoon **on the floor**. __________

c I wiped up the mess **with an old cloth**. __________

d The movie starts **in an hour's time**. __________

e She cut the ribbon **into two halves**. __________

3 Complete the phrase with a preposition.

a I left my hat __________ home.

b We traveled to Chicago plane.

c Tomorrow I have to go __________ the dentist.

d They delivered our furniture __________ the morning.

L.2.1 Demonstrate command of the conventions of standard English grammar and usage when writing or speaking.

Week 31 Day 1 Comprehension

The Fox and the Grapes

Finding the main idea

The main idea of a text is its key point. It sums up what the text is about. Details in the text can help you find the main idea.

Read the passage.

Circle words that describe the **fox**.

Color the fox's **dialogue**.

Underline words that describe the **grapes**.

A hungry fox was looking for food. She saw bunches of juicy, plump grapes growing high up on a farmer's fence.

"I will have those grapes. I'm starving!" she said.

Circle the correct answers.

1 Which **best** describes the main idea of the text?

a A fox wanted to become a farmer.

b A farmer was growing juicy, plump grapes.

c A greedy farmer put food too high for the fox.

d A hungry fox was looking for food.

2 Which **two** text details **support** the main idea?

a growing high up

b hungry fox

c plump grapes

d I'm starving!

3 Which **best** describes what the fox plans to do?

a Steal the fence.

b Eat the grapes.

c Starve the farmer.

d Grow grapes.

The Fox and the Grapes

Read the passage.

The fox ran at the fence and leaped as high as she could. It was a great leap—but it wasn't high enough. She hadn't even reached the lowest bunch of grapes.

The fox tried again. She ran and leaped and it was another wonderful leap. But once again, she did not jump high enough to reach the fruit. She didn't give up though.

Circle **two verbs** that tell how the fox moved.

Underline **adjectives** that describe the leaps.

Box **what** the fox was trying to reach.

1. What is the **main idea**?
   - a The fox wanted the grapes.
   - b The fox tried unsuccessfully to reach the grapes.
   - c The fox refused to give up.

2. Which **two details** helped you find the main idea?
   - a The fox leaped
   - b The fox tried

RL.2.2 Recount stories, including fables and folktales from diverse cultures, and determine their central message, lesson, or moral.

Week 31 Day 3 Spelling

Endings: ar, er, or

Many words that end in **ar**, **er**, and **or** have a similar end sound; e.g., sug**ar**, butt**er**, doct**or**.

1 Copy each list word.

sugar	gather	cracker
butter	number	saucer
doctor	pepper	wander
finger	dollar	tractor
enter	brother	together
dinner	mirror	another
spider	sister	

2 Name.

a

t ______

b

s ______

c

d ______

d

s ______

3 Write the list word that belongs in each group.

a lunch, breakfast, ______

b wafer, cookie, ______

c sister, mother, ______

d plate, dish, ______

e hand, palm, ______

f field, crops, ______

4 Unscramble the letters to make a list word.

a teren ______

b thertoge ______

c rormir ______

d therano ______

e derwan ______

f perpep ______

L.2.2 Demonstrate command of the conventions of standard English capitalization, punctuation, and spelling when writing.

Endings: ar, er, or

1 Underline the spelling mistake. Write the word correctly.

a The docter gave Isha some medicine. ______

b Michael set the salt and peppor on the table. ______

c I found a doller in the pocket of my jeans. ______

d I found him looking at his reflection in the mirrar. ______

e We were told not to wandor off without mom. ______

Challenge words

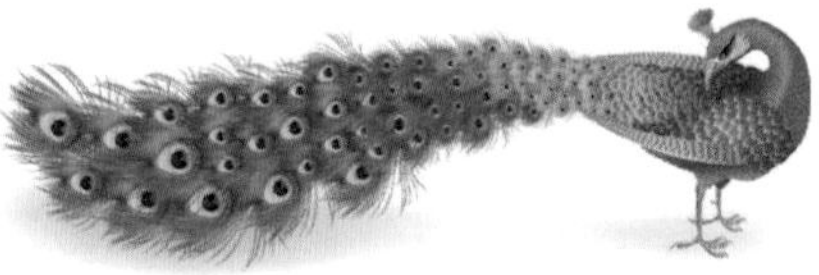

2 Copy each challenge word.

answer ______	October ______
feather ______	November ______
deliver ______	cellar ______
lawyer ______	alligator ______
September ______	caterpillar ______

3 Read the clue. Complete the sentence with a challenge word.

a I look like a crocodile. I am an ______.

b August is before me and October is after me. I am ______.

c I am the second last month of the year. I am ______.

d I am found on birds. I am a ______.

4 Use as many list words as possible to make a silly story.

L.2.2 Demonstrate command of the conventions of standard English capitalization, punctuation, and spelling when writing.

Simple sentences

A **sentence** is a group of words that makes complete sense; e.g., **I am eating breakfast**.
A simple sentence has one **subject** (the person or thing doing the action) and one **verb** (the action); e.g., **The boy** (subject) **is helping** (verb) his friend.

1 Check (✓) the sentences.

a ☐ The children are playing baseball.

b ☐ in the house near the beach

c ☐ past the castle and up the hill

d ☐ I am walking towards the castle.

e ☐ There's a lamp next to my bed.

2 Add extra information to each sentence.

I wore my new costume *to the party.*

a She dropped the ball ________________.

b Noah read the story ________________.

c Marie drew a picture ________________.

d They wrote their names ________________.

3 Write each sentence as a question.

I have read that book. *Have you read that book?*

a They are having lunch.

Are ________________.

b The monkey is swinging in the tree.

Is ________________.

Wet

Visualization

Good readers imagine pictures when they read a text. This is called visualizing. Looking for key words in the text helps you create the images.

Read the passage.

Color **where** tigers live.

Box a word that **describes** a tiger's coat.

Underline **why** a tiger's prey doesn't hear it coming.

Bengal Tigers

Some Bengal tigers live in the mangrove forests of India and Bangladesh.

Tigers hunt mammals, such as wild boars. Bengal tigers also eat saltwater crabs and fish.

Tigers are quick and powerful hunters. They have soft foot pads that help them quietly stalk prey. Their striped coats help them hide in the forest. Every tiger has a different pattern of stripes.

Circle the correct answers.

1. **Where** do Bengal tigers live?
   - a at the park
   - b in the snow
   - c by the ocean
   - d in the forest

2. **Why** might tigers be difficult to spot?
   - a Tigers' stripes help camouflage them.
   - b Tigers hunt at night and sleep all day.
   - c Tigers have excellent eyesight.
   - d Tigers have soft foot pads.

3. Draw three things Bengal tigers eat.

RI.2.1 Ask and answer such questions as who, what, where, when, why, and how to demonstrate understanding of key details in a text.

Wet

Read the full text

Read the passage.

Color where hippos live.

Box **how** a hippo moves.

Underline **what** is on top of a hippo's head.

Hippopotamuses

Hippos live in swampy lakes and rivers in Africa.

Hippos spend the day in the water. A hippo's eyes, ears, and nostrils are on the top of its head. It can watch for danger while the rest of its body is underwater.

Hippos nurse their young and even sleep underwater. Hippos do not truly swim. They run or walk along the river bed.

Hippos are often aggressive. They open their mouths to warn off intruders.

1. Draw and label a picture of a hippo based on information in this text. You can make connections to hippos you've read about in stories, seen on safari, or at the zoo.

Digraphs: ai, a-e

Two letters that make a single sound are called a **digraph**. The **letters ai** make the **single sound ay**; e.g., paid.
When the **digraph ae** is **separated by a consonant**, it becomes a **split digraph**; e.g., lemonade.

1 Copy each list word.

parade ____	grade ____	upgrade ____
paid ____	blade ____	afraid ____
made ____	raid ____	decade ____
wade ____	aid ____	invade ____
maid ____	trade ____	arcade ____
laid ____	shade ____	sunshade ____
fade ____	spade ____	

2 Which list word means?

a someone who is paid to do housework ____
b ten years ____
c a tool used for digging ____
d to give help to someone in need ____
e a sudden surprise attack ____

3 Complete the list words.

a in _ _ d _ b b _ _ de c wad _
d sunsh _ _ _ e tra _ _ f ar _ _ d _

4 Write the list words in alphabetical order.

____ ____ ____ ____

L.2.2 Demonstrate command of the conventions of standard English capitalization, punctuation, and spelling when writing.

Digraphs: ai, a-e

Challenge words

1 Copy each challenge word.

cascade ____________
braid ____________
unafraid ____________
grenade ____________
mermaid ____________
lemonade ____________
bridesmaid ____________
persuade ____________
repaid ____________
marmalade ____________

2 Color the correct word.

a I plaited her long hair into a [braid] [breid].

b Tim spread [marmelaid] [marmalade] on his toast.

c My sister will be a [bridesmeid] [bridesmaid] at our cousin's wedding.

d I poured everyone a cool glass of [lemonaid] [lemonade].

e Cherry tried to [persuade] [persuad] her mother to buy ice cream.

3 Which challenge word means?

a a small waterfall ____________

b a small bomb thrown by hand ____________

c talk someone into ____________

Punctuate simple sentences

A **sentence** starts with a **capital letter**. It ends with a **period**, **question mark**, or **exclamation point**; e.g., **T**he book is on the shelf**.** **W**here is the book**?** **W**hat a great book that was**!**

1 Fill in the missing end punctuation.

a My favorite color is blue

b Which bike is yours

c What a crazy idea

d An octopus has eight tentacles

e Where do you live

2 Check (✓) the sentences that have the correct punctuation.

a ☐ He is putting on his shoes.

b ☐ where are my red socks.

c ☐ What a great time we had!

d ☐ I have lost my mittens?

e ☐ When does it start?

3 Write each sentence using the correct punctuation.

a i have a dog and a cat

____

____

b how old are you today

____

____

L.2.2 Demonstrate command of the conventions of standard English capitalization, punctuation, and spelling when writing.

Week 33 Day 1 Comprehension

Farms

Compare and contrast

When you compare and contrast information, you look for **similarities** and **differences**.

Read the passage.

Vegetables

Many vegetables need a certain temperature to grow well. Some vegetables that grow well in cooler weather are carrots, onions, and winter lettuce. Tomatoes, corn, and peppers need hot, sunny weather to grow well.

Some vegetables, such as lettuce and peppers, are quick growing. Lettuce is ready to eat in six to eight weeks. Other vegetables, such as carrots, tomatoes, onions, and corn take four to five months to grow and ripen.

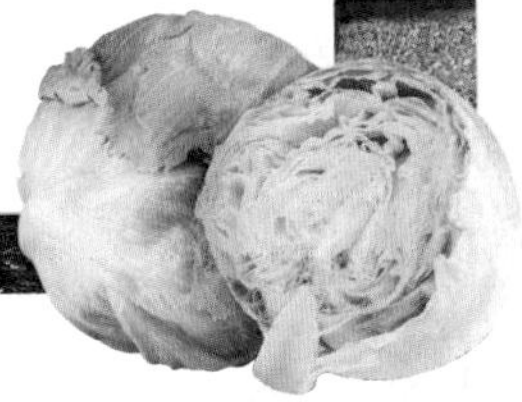

1 Complete the table using ticks [✔].

Vegetable	Grows best in cooler weather	Grows best in warmer weather	Quick to grow	Longer to grow
carrot				
corn				
pepper				
onion				
winter lettuce				
tomato				

2 Put a [✔] next to true information.

a ☐ Carrots and corn are quick-growing vegetables.

b ☐ Onions and tomatoes are best to grow in winter.

c ☐ Peppers are quick-growing vegetables that like warm weather.

d ☐ You would have more tomatoes and corn in summer than in winter.

e ☐ Winter lettuce likes cool weather.

Farms

Read the passage.

Box **what** farmers use **cows** for.

Underline the name for a **group of cows.**

Color **what** farmers use **sheep** for.

Circle the name for a **group of sheep.**

Cows and Sheep

Some farmers raise large herds of cattle. Others raise large flocks of sheep.

Farmers raise herds of cows, called cattle, for their meat and hides. Leather is made into shoes, clothes, and furniture. Cattle eat grass in fields or are fed hay and grain.

Dairy cows make milk. Milk can be made into cheese, yogurt, and ice cream.

Farmers raise sheep for their wool, meat, and milk. Farmers shear sheep once a year. The wool can be made into sweaters, blankets, and carpets.

1. Use the information in the text to compare and contrast sheep and cattle.

Compare and contrast products we get from sheep and cattle.

Sheep	Sheep and Cattle	Cattle

RI.2.6 Identify the main purpose of a text, including what the author wants to answer, explain, or describe.

Word building

New words are formed by adding **prefixes**; e.g., **un**happy, or **suffixes**; e.g., try, try**ing**, tri**ed**.

1 Copy each list word.

law		fright	
lawful		frighten	
unlawful		frightened	
try		happily	
trying		happiness	
tried		happiest	
watch		begin	
watching		beginning	
watched		beginner	
watchful		began	

2 Add suffixes to build words.

	happy	watch	begin
a			
b			
c			

3 Complete each sentence with a list word.

a The thief was arrested for breaking the ____________.

b It is ____________ to steal from other people.

c The loud thunder gave me a ____________.

d I am ____________ of large spiders.

e My brother is ____________ cartoons in the den.

Word building

1 Unscramble the letters to make a list word.

a chedwat ______________ b chfulwat ______________

c inesshapp ______________ d inningbeg ______________

e innerbeg ______________ f ghtfri ______________

Challenge words

2 Copy each challenge word.

garden ______________ decision ______________

gardening ______________ friend ______________

gardener ______________ friendly ______________

decide ______________ friendliness ______________

deciding ______________ unfriendly ______________

3 Complete each sentence with a challenge word.

a Lin is helping plant vegetables in the community ______________.

b Shay and Mat are still ______________ which movie to see.

c The ______________ was not happy with the state of her roses.

d Our new neighbor did not seem to be very ______________.

e I couldn't ______________ which book I liked better.

4 Use as many challenge words as possible to make a silly story.

____

____

____

Conjunctions

A **conjunction** joins single words in sentences; e.g, Alex **and** Isabella are twins. It also joins parts of a sentence; e.g., I bought a hamburger, **but** I didn't eat it.

1 Complete each sentence with a conjunction from the box. Use each conjunction once.

so
but
because
or
and

a Ask either Lucy ____________ Sarah to help you.

b I eat lots of fruit ______________ vegetables.

c I was feeling sick, ______________ I stayed in bed.

d I went for a swim ____________________ I was hot.

e I switched on the engine, _____________ nothing happened.

2 Circle the correct word.

a There were men, women, (because, and, but) children at the concert.

b I practiced the dance (because, until, or) I got tired.

c I put on a jacket (because, but, until) it was cold.

d The bus was full, (or, until, so) I waited for the next one.

e You can have a milkshake (or, but, so) an ice cream, (or, so, but) you can't have both.

3 Write endings for the following sentences.

a I like apples and ____.

b I looked under my bed, but ____

____.

c I dropped the box because ____

____.

Fighter Planes

Sequencing events
To identify the sequence of events in a text, look at words that give clues to the order in which things happen.

Read the passage.

Box **what** gets a plane off the ground.

How a jet engine works

Jet engines burn a mixture of fuel and air. This makes hot gases, which give thrust. Thrust gets a plane off the ground and keeps it moving.

Underline **how** hot gases are made.

1 What does a jet engine burn?

a thrust and ground
b fuel and air
c gases and thrust
d jets and air

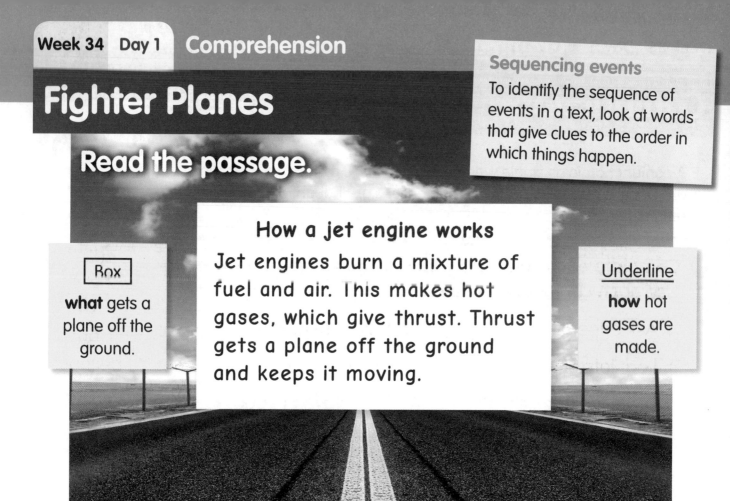

2 Order the events using the numbers 1-5.

☐ The hot gases give thrust.
☐ Thrust lifts a plane off the ground
☐ Jet engines burn a mixture of fuel and air.
☐ Thrust keeps the fighter plane moving.
☐ The mix of fuel and air makes hot gases.

RI.2.3 Describe the connection between a series of historical events, scientific ideas or concepts, or steps in technical procedures in a text.

Fighter Planes

Read the full text

Read the passage.

Color **what** helps a plane get off the ground.

Underline a **type** of fighter plane.

Swing Wings

Wide wings help get a plane off the ground. They also slow it down in the sky. Swing wings solve this problem. On fighters like the F-14 Tomcat, the wings sweep back once the jet is in the air.

1. **What** helps a plane take off?

   ____

2. On an F-14 Tomcat, **where** are the wings at take-off?

   ____

3. On an F-14 Tomcat, **when** do the wings sweep back?

   ____

4. **What** do you predict will happen to the wings when it is time to land?

   ____

Suffixes: er, est

Add the **suffixes er** or **est** to adjectives that compare two or more items. If the adjective ends in a consonant after a short vowel, double the consonant before adding **er** or **est**; e.g., big → bi**gg**er → bi**gg**est.
If the adjective ends in y, change the y to i before adding **er** or **est**; e.g., smelly → smell**i**er → smell**i**est.

1 Copy each list word.

bigger		happier	
biggest		happiest	
fattest		healthier	
tinier		healthiest	
tiniest		angrier	
easier		angriest	
easiest		flatter	
saddest		busiest	
heavier		funnier	
heaviest		funniest	

2 Sort the list words.

Suffixes: er, est

1 Complete each sentence with a list word.

a The elephant is ________________ than the zebra.

b That was the ________________ joke I have ever heard.

c The blue whale is the ________________ animal in the world.

d That was the ________________ karate competition we've done this year.

e I am ________________ when I am with my friends.

Challenge words

2 Copy each challenge word.

dirtiest	________________	smelliest	________________
tidier	________________	thinnest	________________
fittest	________________	scariest	________________
dimmer	________________	fluffier	________________
dirtier	________________	curliest	________________

3 Complete each sentence with a challenge word.

a The orange kitten's fur is ________________ than the black kitten's fur.

b This light bulb is ________________ than that one.

c Her hair is by far the ________________ I have ever seen!

d Mark's room is ________________ than mine.

4 Color the correct word.

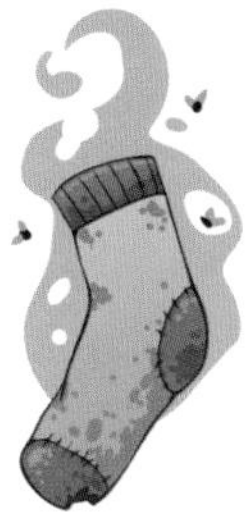

a I found the [smelliest] [smeliest] sock in my brother's swim bag.

b She made me watch the [scarist] [scariest] movie!

c I snapped the [thinnest] [thinest] branch.

Compound sentences

A **compound sentence** is a sentence with more than one verb. When we join two simple sentences with the conjunctions **and**, **or**, **but**, or **so,** we make a compound sentence; e.g., Ella drew. James painted. Ella drew **and** James painted.

1 Complete each sentence with a conjunction from the box.

and	or
but	so

a They got in the car __________ drove off.

b It was getting dark, __________ I went inside.

c Jack's birthday is in May __________ Gina's is in June.

d We can go to the movies, __________ we can go to the beach.

e I looked in my room, __________ my kitten wasn't there.

2 Color the conjunction and underline the verbs.

a Jemma fed the dogs, and Miles bathed them.

b Amelia packed her bag, but she left it at home.

c It was very hot, so I stayed indoors.

d Drink the juice immediately, or put it in the fridge.

3 Join the two sentences with the conjunction.

a Max plays basketball. Abby plays baseball. (and)

____

____

b Jackson is tall. Joshua is taller. (but)

____

____

L.2.1.F Produce, expand, and rearrange complete compound sentences.

Healthy Eating

Compare and contrast
To compare and contrast information, look for the **similarities** and **differences** between details in the text.

Read the passage.

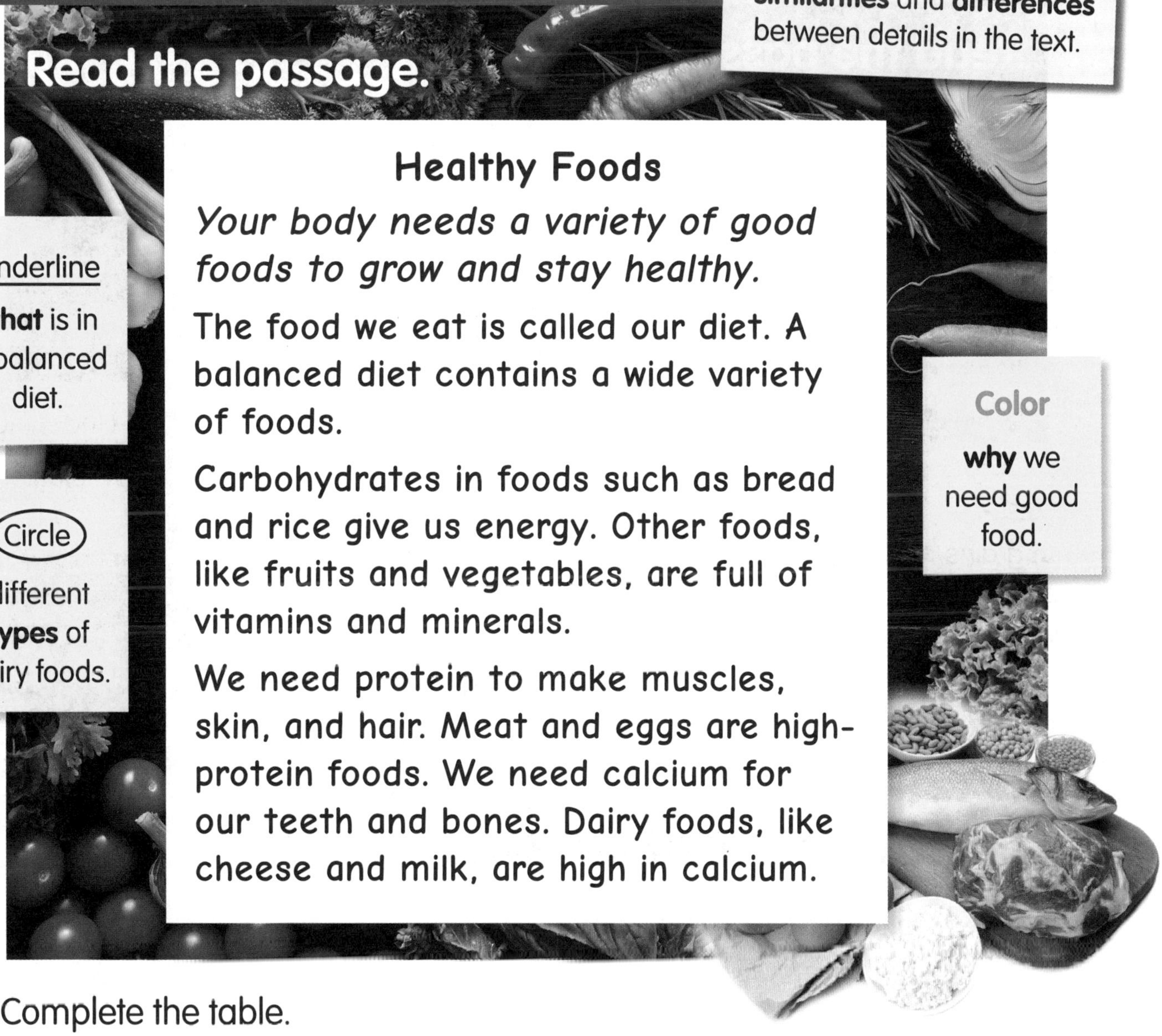

Underline **what** is in a balanced diet.

Circle different **types** of dairy foods.

Color **why** we need good food.

Healthy Foods

Your body needs a variety of good foods to grow and stay healthy.

The food we eat is called our diet. A balanced diet contains a wide variety of foods.

Carbohydrates in foods such as bread and rice give us energy. Other foods, like fruits and vegetables, are full of vitamins and minerals.

We need protein to make muscles, skin, and hair. Meat and eggs are high-protein foods. We need calcium for our teeth and bones. Dairy foods, like cheese and milk, are high in calcium.

1 Complete the table.

	Why we need them	Examples
Carbohydrates		
Fruit and vegetables		
Protein		
Dairy		

Healthy Eating

Read the passage.

Grains

A healthy diet should include grains, such as wheat, rice, and corn.

Some grain is cooked and eaten whole. These are wholegrain foods. Other grain is ground into flour to make bread, pasta, and cereals. All grains have carbohydrates, which give the body energy.

Some wholegrain foods are corn on the cob, rice, and wholegrain bread. They are high in fiber. Wholegrains contain magnesium, a mineral that helps build strong bones and teeth.

Box **what** can be made with grains.

Circle **what** grains give the body.

Underline wholegrain foods.

1. What do all grains give the body?

____

2. What extra nutrients do wholegrains give the body?

____

____

3. What is magnesium good for?

____

____

RI.2.8 Describe how reasons support specific points the author makes in a text.

Week 35 Day 3 Spelling

Tricky words

Some words are trickier to spell than others. Not all words follow the rules. Some have letters that are not supposed to be there. Some leave out letters. Some have letters in the wrong order.

1 Copy each list word.

I ______	with ______	pretty ______
again ______	there ______	who ______
always ______	off ______	mother ______
next ______	here ______	father ______
have ______	around ______	outside ______
were ______	wanted ______	when ______
things ______	school ______	

2 Which list word means?

a a place for teaching and learning ______

b any space that is not inside ______

c a female parent ______

d a male parent ______

3 Write the opposite.

a on ______

b unwanted ______

c ugly ______

d without ______

e inside ______

f never ______

4 Complete each sentence with a list word.

a Our neighbors ______ a huge trampoline.

b I took ______ my shoes before entering the house.

c We spun ______ in circles.

d We need to get off at the ______ bus stop.

Tricky words

1 Underline the spelling mistake. Write the word correctly.

a Ie am seven years old. ____________

b Mom told us to play outsde in the garden. ____________

c I wantid a new computer, but I got a book instead. ____________

d I went to the zoo weth my grandma and grandpa. ____________

e I got it wrong, so I had to start all over agein. ____________

Challenge words

2 Copy each challenge word.

every	____________	children	____________
once	____________	people	____________
happening	____________	swimming	____________
scared	____________	women	____________
favorite	____________	February	____________

3 Complete each sentence with a challenge word.

a The ____________ were excited to play in the snow.

b On hot days we like to go ____________ in the pool.

c My birthday is in ____________, the second month of the year.

d Chocolate is my ____________ flavor of ice cream.

e I am ____________ of big hairy spiders.

4 Use as many challenge words as possible to make a silly sentence.

____

____

L.2.2 Demonstrate command of the conventions of standard English capitalization, punctuation, and spelling when writing.

Capitalizing proper nouns

The names of particular **places**, **holidays**, and **products** are **proper nouns**; e.g., **M**exico, **H**alloween, **M**icrosoft. All of the words in a proper noun start with a capital letter; e.g., **N**ew **Y**ork, **G**olden **G**ate **B**ridge.

1 Circle the word that needs a capital letter.

a river amazon

b everest mountain

c holiday thanksgiving

d smartphone apple

e city pittsburg

f canada country

2 Color the words that need a capital letter.

a The grand canyon is in the state of arizona.

b We have two cars—a ford and a toyota.

c My cousin goes to ravenscliff elementary school.

d Many people wear green on saint patrick's day.

e I have never been to europe, africa, or south america.

3 Write this sentence with the correct capitalization.

My best friend lives in simpson street.

Clothes

Making inferences

Use **clues** in the text to make inferences. The clues will help you find the answers that are hiding in the text.

Read the passage.

Circle **when** machinery for making clothes was invented.

Box **the adjective** that describes clothes of the 1800s.

Underline **the invention** that led to clothes being mass-produced.

1800s

During the 1800s, machinery for making clothes was invented. More factories were built. Textiles became mass-produced.

Before machinery, weavers and tailors made clothes by hand.

Sewing machines were invented and then mass-produced during the 1800s. This allowed women at home to make clothing quickly and easily. Clothes of the 1800s were often uncomfortable to wear. Women wore bone corsets that laced up tightly.

Circle the correct answer/s.

1. Which **best** describes the big change in the clothing industry in the 1800s?
   - a Machinery was used to make clothes.
   - b Sewing machines were affordable but uncomfortable.
   - c Women liked to make fashionable clothing.
   - d Men made clothes.

2. Which **clues** tell you this?
   - a Women wore bone corsets that laced up tightly.
   - b During the 1800s, machinery for making clothes was invented.
   - c More factories were built.
   - d Clothes of the 1800s were often uncomfortable to wear.
   - e Sewing machines were invented and then mass-produced during the 1800s.
   - f This allowed women at home to make clothing quickly and easily.

RI.2.8 Describe how reasons support specific points the author makes in a text.

Clothes

Read the passage.

Underline popular clothes in the 1990s.

Box the description of **bathing suits**.

1990s

During the 1990s, people wore shirts, hats, and sunglasses to protect against skin cancer.

Hats were not popular in the 1970s and 1980s. In the 1990s, people became more aware of skin cancer. Hats became common again.

Many bathing suits, especially for young children, once again covered much of the body. This was to protect them from the sun.

1. Draw people dressed for the beach in the 1970s and 1990s.

1970s	1990s

Suffixes: ment, ness

Adding the **suffix ment** to a verb turns it into a noun; e.g., enjoy**ment**. Adding the **suffix ness** to an adjective turns it into a noun; e.g., weak**ness**.

1 Copy each list word.

illness ____________	laziness ____________
payment ____________	fairness ____________
sadness ____________	enjoyment ____________
darkness ____________	thickness ____________
fitness ____________	blackness ____________
sickness ____________	amusement ____________
richness ____________	movement ____________
neatness ____________	statement ____________
weakness ____________	amazement ____________
softness ____________	treatment ____________

2 Complete the list word.

a fit _ _ _ _ b enjoy _ _ _ _ c soft _ _ _ _

d thick _ _ _ _ e black _ _ _ _ f dark _ _ _ _

3 Unscramble these list words.

a ntmepay ____________ b ntmeeattr ____________

c nessfair ____________ d momevent ____________

e ntmemusea ____________ f menteamaz ____________

4 Underline the spelling mistake. Write the word correctly.

a I felt sadnes when my friend moved away. ____________

b I turned on a light to see in the darknes. ____________

c The crowd looked on in amazment. ____________

L.2.2 Demonstrate command of the conventions of standard English capitalization, punctuation, and spelling when writing.

Suffixes: ment, ness

Challenge words

1 Copy each challenge word.

argument	______	punishment	______
excitement	______	astonishment	______
gentleness	______	equipment	______
willingness	______	tiredness	______
entertainment	______	enchantment	______

2 Complete each sentence with a challenge word.

a My brother and I always have an ______ about who sits in the front seat.

b Dad made us scrub the floor as ______ for our bad behavior.

c When camping, you must remember to bring the right ______.

d Thinking about our European vacation filled me with ______.

3 Color the correct word.

a It was her [willingness] [wilngess] to learn that made her a good team player.

b We stared in [astonesment] [astonishment] at our coach's strange hat.

c They hired a clown as [entertainment] [enterteinmnt] for the party.

Formal and informal language

Informal language is usually used when speaking or writing emails to friends and family; e.g., **Hi** Jerry. Formal language is used when speaking to older people, especially if we do not know them very well; e.g., **Good morning**, Mr. Clarke.

1 In each pair, color the more informal expression.

a thank you / thanks

b won't / will not

c yes / yeah

d cinema / movies

e do not know / dunno

f child / kid

2 In each pair, color the more formal expression.

a y'all / everybody

b very good / awesome

c delicious / yummy

d would have / would've

e What is the matter? / What's up?

f quite soon / pretty soon

3 Rewrite the sentence so that it sounds more formal.

You wanna come with me? *Would you like to come with me?*

I ain't ever been to Washington D.C.

____

____

Spelling

Use this review to test your knowledge. It has three parts Spelling, Grammar, and Comprehension. If you're unsure of an answer, go back and read the rules and generalizations in the blue boxes.

You have learned about:

- irregular past tense verbs
- endings: ar, er, or
- suffixes: er, est
- split digraphs
- digraphs: ai, a-e
- tricky words
- digraphs: ea, ee
- word building
- suffixes: ment, less

1 Complete each word with one of these. 2 marks

ai ee a-e i-e

a sk__t__ b sm__l__ c sh__ __t d afr__ __d

2 Which word completes the sentence? 1 mark

On Saturday, I ____________ to the zoo.

a go b went c goes d going

3 Add suffixes to build words with happy. 3 marks

a happy + ly = ____________

b happy + ness = ____________

c happy + est = ____________

4 Complete the words with or, er, or ar. 2 marks

a sauc__ __ b doll__ __ c fing__ __ d tract__ __

5 Which word completes the sentence? 1 mark

The buffalo was ____________ than the antelope.

a heaviest b heavy c heavily d heavier

6 Underline the word spelled incorrectly. Write it correctly. 1 mark

I've allways wanted to be an astronaut. ____________

Your score

/10

Grammar

You have learned about:

- irregular verbs
- prepositions
- adverbial phrases
- simple sentences
- punctuating sentences
- conjunctions
- compound sentences
- proper nouns
- formal and informal language

1 Write the verbs in brackets in the past tense. 3 marks

a Last night I (eat) ______________ all my dinner.

b This morning I (drink) ______________ a glass of milk.

c Last week Simon (bring) ______________ his dog to basketball practice.

2 Circle the correct preposition. 2 marks

a The toy was spinning (around, on) the room.

b I dipped my toes (in, over) the water.

3 Complete the phrase with a preposition. 2 marks

a The librarian greeted us ______________ a smile.

b Birds build their nests ______________ trees.

4 In each sentence, circle the verb. 2 marks

a The cow sat quietly under a tree.

b The dogs dug holes in the garden.

Grammar

5 Write each sentence with the correct punctuation. 2 marks

a she has lost her keys ______________________________

____

b what are they doing ______________________________

____

6 Complete each sentence with a conjunction from the box. Use each conjunction once. 4 marks

so because or but

a I have to wash my hands ______________ they are sticky.

b I have eaten my lunch, ______________ I am still hungry.

c I was hungry, ______________ I made myself a sandwich.

d You can sit, ______________ you can stand.

7 Join the two sentences with the conjunction.

Becky has a white cat. Lucy has a black cat. (and) 1 mark

____

____

8 Color the words that need a capital letter. 2 marks

a We celebrated independence day in miami.

b We bought our fridge at walmart.

9 In each pair, color the more formal expression. 2 marks

a Hi Good morning

b How R U? How are you?

Your score

/20

How Can We Attract Birds into Our Gardens?

Read the passage and then use the comprehension skills you have learned to answer the questions.

According to Professor Scott, one way we shouldn't be attracting birds into our gardens is by feeding them. The large number of birds around a bird feeder attracts cats. Also, larger birds start to take over the area while some, like crows, attack the smaller birds and eat their eggs and chicks.

Another reason for not feeding birds is that sometimes they become so used to getting food from us that they stop looking for food in the wild. In addition, the food we give them is often not the right kind and can make them ill.

Professor Scott says the best way to attract birds into our gardens is to create a wild area with native plants in it. The birds will come into the garden to feed on the pollen, seeds, and fruit of these plants. They will also eat the insects in the area. In this way, they will eat their natural foods.

We should also make sure there is fresh water for the birds, and we should definitely avoid using chemicals on the plants.

1. Why do people keep bird feeders in their gardens? 1 mark **LITERAL**

   a to attract cats b to attract birds

   c to make sure birds don't starve d as ornaments

2. Why would cats be attracted to birds around a bird feeder? Cats ... 1 mark **INFERENTIAL**

   a prey on birds. b play with birds.

   c like to watch birds. d steal the birds' food.

How Can We Attract Birds into Our Gardens?

3 Which of the following is a big bird? 1 mark **INFERENTIAL**

a a blue jay b a sparrow c a finch d a crow

4 Who is Professor Scott? Professor Scott is most likely a ... 1 mark **INFERENTIAL**

a scientist. b farmer. c reporter. d photographer.

5 Which is a reason for not feeding birds? If we feed birds, they could ... 1 mark **LITERAL**

a get fat. b frighten our pets.

c stop coming into our gardens. d get sick.

6 What part of a native tree do birds not eat? 1 mark **INFERENTIAL**

a leaves b pollen c seeds d fruit

7 Which word is the opposite of *native* in the phrase *native* plants? 1 mark **VOCABULARY**

a local b alien c natural d wild

8 Why does Professor Scott say we shouldn't use chemicals on plants? The chemicals might ... 1 mark **INFERENTIAL**

a kill the plants. b improve the soil.

c get washed away by rain. d poison the birds.

9 What is the purpose of the text? 1 mark **CRITICAL**

a to retell an event b to give advice

c to tell a story d to explain how something works

10 Who is the target audience for this text? People who ... 1 mark **CRITICAL**

a live in the city. b have big gardens.

c want more birds in their gardens. d have cats.

Your score ☐ /10

Your Review 4 Scores

Spelling		Grammar		Comprehension		Total
☐ /10	+	☐ /20	+	☐ /10	=	☐ /40

Week 1, Day 1
Pg 2

Answers to passage will vary. Talk through responses.

1 b **2** a **3** a **4** b **5** a

Week 1, Day 2
Pg 3

A Gecko on the Teacher!

The gecko jumps onto Mr. Mooney's hand. It runs up his arm. It leaps onto his head and waves at us.

Mr. Mooney's eyes roll up and his mouth is the shape of an O.

His arms freeze halfway to his head, as if he's too afraid to move.

1 running up Mr. Mooney's arm to his head

2 scared, afraid

3 *Answers will vary. Suggested answer:* I was surprised when my parents took me to camp in Yosemite National Park with my cousins.

Week 1, Day 3
Pg 4

1 Check for correct spelling of each word.

2 a dancess dances **b** listenes listens **c** breakes breaks **d** buyes buys

3 a crosses **b** covers **c** melts **d** behaves **e** coaches **f** hammers

4 a melts **b** dances **c** breaks

Week 1, Day 4
Pg 5

1

break	breaks
push	pushes
bite	bites
grow	grows

2 Check for correct spelling of each word.

3 *Answers will vary. Read through the story together.*

4 a finishes **b** measures **c** vanishes **d** teaches **e** switches

Week 1, Day 5
Pg 6

1 a hat **b** sun **c** pig **d** cyclist **e** house

2 a thing **b** person **c** animal **d** place

3 a moon **b** star

4 a ant **b** dull

Week 2, Day 1
Pg 7

A Good Idea

"Haven't you ever seen a money tree?" asked Mandy.

Tim shook his head. "How do people get a money tree?"

"Easy!" Mandy laughed. "They plant a coin in a pot full of dirt. Then they water it."

"When the coin grows into a tree, flowers grow on it. The flowers turn into money," she told him.

1 a

2 b

3 c

Week 2, Day 2
Pg 8

Trouble!

Mom didn't like Mandy playing tricks on Tim.

"There's only one thing to do," Mom said. "Take the coins out of your piggybank and stick them on Tim's tree."

"But I was saving up to buy a book!" Mandy told her.

1 Mandy

2 to take the coins out of her piggybank and give them to Tim

3 she played a trick on Tim

4 a book

Week 2, Day 3
Pg 9

1 Check for correct spelling of each word.

2 a worm **b** shark **c** arm **d** storm

3 ar words: arm, warm, ward, shark, warp, spark, war, car, warn, wart, apart
or words: worm, word, storm, snort, stork, work, born, short, sport

Week 2, Day 4
Pg 10

1 a warm **b** sport **c** car **d** shark **e** wart

2 Check for correct spelling of each word.

3 *Answers will vary. Suggested answer:* to, war, dot, raw, ward, toad, row, wart, tow, road

4 a morning **b** wharf **c** corner **d** toward

Week 2, Day 5
Pg 11

1 a flock **b** pride **c** pair **d** pod **e** swarm **f** fleet

2 a litter **b** school **c** band

3 a gang/thieves **b** library/books **c** bunch/flowers

Week 3, Day 1
Pg 12

Happy Birds

Lots of cages hung in the trees. Grandpa hung Yan's cage with the others.

There were lots of grandpas and lots of songbirds. All the birds whistled.

The air was full of whistles. Grandpa sat on a bench and whistled too.

Yan liked to sing with the other birds. Grandpa liked to whistle with the other grandpas.

1 d **2** c **3** a

Week 3, Day 2
Pg 13

Dear Grandpa,

The birds in Australia have bright feathers. Some are gray and pink. Others are white and wear yellow hats. They all sing very loudly.

I wish you could hear the birds, Grandpa. They are happy birds. I am sure Yan would be happy in Australia. You would be happy too.

I miss going to the park with you, Grandpa.

Love, Ling

1 Ling says they are bright, colourful and happy

2 yes: Ling says Australian birds are happy, Yan and Grandpa would be happy, and that she misses going to the park with him

Week 3, Day 3
Pg 14

1 Check for correct spelling of each word.

2 a hockey **b** money **c** ninety **d** pretty **e** honey **f** turkey

3 a turkey **b** money **c** donkey **d** key

4 a mony money **b** ninty ninety **c** hocky hockey

Week 3, Day 4
Pg 15

1 any, donkey, empty, fairy, ugly
2 Check for correct spelling of each word.
3 a chimney **b** January **c** library **d** parsley **e** family
4 a jersey **b** February **c** library **d** country

Week 3, Day 5
Pg 16

1 a Check for correct name
b Check for correct month
c December
d Check for correct name
e Abraham
2 Monday, Tuesday, Wednesday, Thursday, Friday, Saturday, Sunday
3 a ben Ben **b** bailey Bailey **c** august August **d** brown Brown **e** hilda Hilda

Week 4, Day 1
Pg 17

More Unusual Pets

A goose flew in through the window. She landed with a thump. She grumbled as she got up off the floor.

Then a hyena came to the door. He had the hiccups. He saw the goose and laughed.

They began to argue. It went on and on until Stella yelled, "Stop!"

The room was silent. The crocodile stood very still.

1 b **2** c

Week 4, Day 2
Pg 18

Rabbit Chase

"Help! Help!" yelled the rabbit. "The lion is trying to eat me!"

"I am not," said the lion. He sounded hurt. "I was trying to whisper in your ear. But one of your whiskers tickled my nose. I just slipped.

"Then your foot was in my mouth. I don't know how that happened. Mmmmmm, yummy."

1 lion/rabbit
2 a "Help! Help! The lion is trying to eat me!"
b "Mmmmmm, yummy."

Week 4, Day 3
Pg 19

1 Check for correct spelling of each word.
2 str words: street, strong, strap, strip, struck, stream, streak, stroke, strike, strain, stripe, string, stride
spr words: spray, sprint, spring
scr words: scrub, scrape, screen, scream
3 a stroke **b** street **c** strap

Week 4, Day 4
Pg 20

1 a streng string **b** sprent sprint **c** scren screen **d** strype stripe **e** streem stream
2 Check for correct spelling of each word.
3 a strict **b** stroll **c** screech **d** sprinkle
4 *Answers will vary. Read through the story together.*

Week 4, Day 5
Pg 21

1 a I **b** They **c** him **d** she **e** us
2 a me **b** They **c** you **d** it **e** She
3 a them **b** her **c** him **d** it

Week 5, Day 1
Pg 22

A thirsty ant came to the edge of a river to get a drink. The fast-moving water splashed the ant and knocked it into the river. The ant was in trouble! It tried to swim, but it was drowning.

A dove sitting in a tree picked a leaf and dropped it in the river, near the ant. The ant climbed onto the leaf and floated to safety on the bank of the river.

1 a **2** c, d **3** b

Week 5, Day 2
Pg 23

A little while later, a hunter came to the edge of the river. He saw the dove sitting in the tree and quickly drew his bow and aimed at the resting bird. The ant saw what was about to happen. It ran over to the hunter and bit his toe as hard as it could. The hunter cried out and dropped his bow. The dove was startled and flew away to safety.

1 ant/dove
2 a bit the hunter's toe as hard as he could
b cried out and startled the dove so it could fly away

Week 5, Day 3
Pg 24

1 Check for correct spelling of each word.
2 a quake **b** queen **c** quiver **d** quote **e** quest **f** quiz
3 a queen **b** squeak **c** squirrel **d** quilt **e** quack
4 a quilt **b** queen **c** squirrel

Week 5, Day 4
Pg 25

1 Missing letters are underlined
a equal **b** quit **c** equip **d** quest **e** quite **f** quaint
2 Check for correct spelling of each word.
3 a queasy **b** quench **c** question **d** squelch
4 a frequent **b** squabble **c** question **d** quench **e** squelch

Week 5, Day 5
Pg 26

1 a a **b** an **c** An/an **d** a/a **e** a/an
2 a a **b** a **c** the **d** an **e** the **f** an **g** a
3 a an **b** a **c** an

Week 6, Day 1
Pg 27

Plants in Summer
Plants grow quickly in summer.
Many plants flower in summer. Flowers make seeds. Some flowers, like apple blossoms, become fruit. Fruit grows and ripens in the summer.
In summer, trees are covered in green leaves. The leaves make food for the tree. The trunk grows thicker.

1 a **2** b **3** c

Week 6, Day 2
Pg 28

Summer Food
We eat more fresh food in summer.
Salads are made from fresh summer vegetables. Families enjoy the outdoors by having picnics and barbecues.
Many fruits, such as berries, melons and peaches are ripe in the summer. Fruit salad is good for you and tastes good too.

1 fresh foods
2 vegetables or fruit
3 outdoors
4 berries, melons, and peaches
5 fruit salad

Week 6, Day 3
Pg 29

1 Check for correct spelling of each word.
2 ing words: saving, posing, sharing, writing, hiking, giving, wasting, gazing
ed words: closed, used, chased, changed, phoned, teased, solved, freed, raced, agreed, shaped, exploded
3 a closed **b** sharing **c** hiking
d posing **e** changed **f** freed

Week 6, Day 4
Pg 30

1 a chaased chased
b explooded exploded
c sollved solved
d agred agreed
2 Check for correct spelling of each word.
3 a freezing **b** created **c** arriving
4 *Answers will vary. Read through the story together.*

Week 6, Day 5
Pg 31

1 a the **b** my, i **c** the **d** my
e noah, i
2 a There is someone at the door.
b My sister can play the trumpet.
c My sister and I have our own rooms.
d Our cousins like their new house.
e Emma and I have finished our chores.
3 a The baby is eating his food.
b Ruby and I are sisters.

Week 7, Day 1
Pg 32

Finding Water
Water is hard to find in a dry habitat.
Birds and large mammals, such as antelopes, elephants, and zebras, travel long distances to find water.
Other animals get water from the food they eat. Australian bilbies and kangaroo rats get water from insects, fruit, seeds, and leaves.

1 ✔ a, b, e, f ✘ c, d

Week 7, Day 2
Pg 33

Conserving Water
Desert animals have special water-saving strategies.
Some animals in dry habitats do not sweat to cool down. This helps the kangaroo rat and the fennec fox to conserve water.
Reptiles have thick skins. Spiders and insects have exoskeletons. These hard, outer shells reduce water loss.

1 ✔ a, b, d, f ✘ c, e

Week 7, Day 3
Pg 34

1 Check for correct spelling of each word.
2 a unhappy **b** unroll **c** unable
d unkind **e** unmade **f** unwind
g untrue
3 Missing letters are underlined
a unfair **b** unlike **c** unwise
d unload **e** unsafe **f** unfit
4 a untrue **b** unfold **c** unhappy

Week 7, Day 4
Pg 35

1 Check for correct spelling of each word.
2 *Answers will vary. Suggested answers:* friend, friendly, end, fun, fire, den, nine, dine
3 a unlucky **b** unwrap **c** unfriendly
d unbuckle
4 a unhealthy **b** unhelpful **c** unusual
d untangle

Week 7, Day 5
Pg 36

1 a hot **b** furry **c** six **d** delicious **e** angry
2 How many? twelve, twenty, seven
What color? Blue, brown, purple
What taste? Bitter, sweet, spicy
3 delicious, crispy, round, hot

Week 8, Day 1
Pg 37

Old Trains
The first trains were pulled along by steam engines.
Steam engines burn coal. The burning coal heats water to make steam. The steam makes the wheels turn.
In the 1800s steam trains were a quick and cheap way to travel for fun as well as for work. Today most steam trains are for tourists.

1 c **2** c, d

Week 8, Day 2
Pg 38

New Trains
Today, most trains have diesel or electric engines.
The new engines are quieter and cleaner than coal-powered steam engines. Diesel trains are often used in country areas. Many electric trains run in cities.
Some electric trains can travel very fast. They are called high-speed trains. The bullet trains in Japan can travel three times faster than a car.

1 new trains
2 are diesel or electric.
3 are quieter and cleaner than coal-powered engines.

Week 8, Day 3
Pg 39

1 Check for correct spelling of each word.

2 a tooth **b** igloo **c** foot **d** hook

3 short oo words: hook, foot, wood, took
long oo words: too, mood, room, soon, hoot, cool, tooth, broom, gloom, igloo, goose, proof, shoot, loose, groom, ooze

Week 8, Day 4
Pg 40

1 a room **b** broom **c** igloo

2 Check for correct spelling of each word.

3 a rooster **b** boomerang **c** scooter **d** poodle **e** cocoon

4 a goodbye **b** snooze **c** kangaroo

Week 8, Day 5
Pg 41

1 mice, women, people, oxen

2 a teeth **b** children **c** geese **d** feet **e** women

3 sheep, deer, moose

Week 9, Day 1
Pg 42

1 5, 4, 1, 3, 2

2 *Answers will vary. Suggested answer:* A drawing of seeds in the field with sunshine and/or rain.

Week 9, Day 2
Pg 43

Refining

Trucks carry wheat to flour mills. The wheat grains are made into flour.

People inspect the wheat to make sure it is good quality.

The grain is cleaned and soaked in water for 10 to 20 hours. This separates the outer layer of bran from the soft, inner part. Rollers crush the wheat into a powder called flour.

1 it is cleaned

2 rollers crush the wheat into a powder called flour

3 how to refine wheat

Week 9, Day 3
Pg 44

1 Check for correct spelling of each word.

2 a race **b** face **c** city **d** mice

2 Missing letters are underlined
a lace **b** slice **c** twice **d** ice
e Once **f** nice

Week 9, Day 4
Pg 45

1 a spicy **b** race **c** space **d** city **e** cell

2 Check for correct spelling of each word.

3 a juicy **b** pencil **c** prince **d** fleece **e** piece

4 a fleece **b** pencil **c** prince

Week 9, Day 5
Pg 46

1 a Commas after Tess, friend,
b Comma after Johnson, neighbor,

2 a *Answers will vary.*
b *Answers will vary.*

REVIEW 1
Spelling
Pg 47

1 b

2 c

3 Missing letters are underlined
a street **b** scrub **c** sprint

4 a spicy **b** hockey **c** queasy **d** unhappy

5 *Answers will vary. Suggested answers:* boom, rang, room, bang, room, broom, manor, oar, game, bear, beam, bean, moon, grab

Grammar
Pg 48–49

1 a bird **b** box

2 a herd **b** pod

3 a amy **b** january

4 a she **b** her **c** they **d** them

5 a an, the **b** the, a

6 *Answers will vary. Suggested answer:* My best friend has two dogs.

7 a feet **b** men

8 Commas after Meg, niece,

Comprehension
Pg 50–51

1 c **2** b **3** d **4** c **5** a **6** b
7 d **8** a **9** b **10** c

Week 10, Day 1
Pg 52

Thump! Thump! Thump!

What is that?
"Thump!"
It's coming from the closet. Tim creeps over and slides the door open. A tiny purple alien steps out and pokes Tim on the foot.
"Take me to your weader!"
Tim jumps back on the bed. The alien is only as big as a teddy bear, but he has a zap gun. The gun is pointed at Tim.
"Wha ... what?" Tim asks.

1 a **2** d **3** a

Week 10, Day 2
Pg 53

Slime Jello

"Here is some slime instead," Tim yells.
Gweep looks in the bowl. "This bad."
Tim looks at the yummy, wobbly, green jello. "It's really very nice."
Tears form in Gweep's three round eyes. "It's saying no!"
"The slime isn't saying no. It's shaking because it's scared of you."
"Is it scared?" Gweep smiles.
"Of me?"

1 because it is wobbly and green, just like slime

2 he smiles because he thinks the jello is scared of him

Week 10, Day 3
Pg 54

1 Check for correct spelling of each word.

2 a tries **b** spies **c** hobbies **d** cities **e** carries

3 a fries **b** babies **c** cries

Week 10, Day 4
Pg 55

1 a carries **b** babies **c** stories **d** parties **e** worries **f** studies

2 Check for correct spelling of each word.

3 a injuries **b** difficulties **c** factories **d** multiplies

4 difficulties, enemies, factories, injuries, libraries, memories, multiplies, properties, qualities, supplies

Week 10, Day 5
Pg 56

1 a rides **b** brushes **c** eats **d** skips **e** bakes

2 a cook **b** buys **c** carry **d** writes **e** dives

3 a play/beat **b** write/draw **c** stop **d** hit **e** eat

Week 11, Day 1
Pg 57

Beds Are Not Trampolines

Tim did a star jump. Then he fell off the bed and landed on his nose. He started to cry.

He cried louder and louder. Mom came running into the room and picked him up.

"Now what have you done?" she asked, looking at his red nose.

"Mandy made me do it," Tim sobbed.

1 d **2** b **3** b **4** d

Week 11, Day 2
Pg 58

Big Trouble

Tim was in big trouble. He had climbed out the bedroom window to make a water balloon.

As he turned the water on, his balloon flew off. Water sprayed all over the yard. Just then, Mom and Aunt Beth stepped into the garden. Both of them were sprayed with water. Boy, were they angry!

Answers will vary. Suggested answers:

1 surprised

2 Climbs out the window. Turns on the tap. Balloon sprays water.

3 Drawing with Tim looking surprised, Mom looking angry, and Aunt Beth shocked.

Week 11, Day 3
Pg 59

1 Check for correct spelling of each word.

2 a jewel **b** jump **c** giraffe **d** jug

3 j: jar, jog, jug, joke, jump, jelly, join, June, July, jewel, Japan, adjust, January

g: gem, germ, giant, angel, giraffe, magic, energy

Week 11, Day 4
Pg 60

1 a jump **b** giraffe **c** January **d** jug **e** joke

2 Check for correct spelling of each word.

3 a jacket **b** juice **c** engine **d** jigsaw **e** digit

4 agile, allergy, digit, engine, fragile, jacket, jigsaw, juice, margin, urgent

Week 11, Day 5
Pg 61

1 Present tense: push, sail, fill, play

Past tense: walked, stopped, blamed, picked

2 a fix fixed **b** enter entered **c** finish finished **d** visit visited **e** watch watched

3 a I locked the door to the garage.

b I washed the dishes after dinner.

Week 12, Day 1
Pg 62

Gee-Gee?

When I picked him up, Greedy Guts chewed on my fingers. Then he gnawed the strap of my watch.

I put him on the floor and he untied my shoelaces. Then he tried to pull my left sock off. He loved me so much, he wanted to eat me. How could I resist him?

"Mom, please," I begged. "He's perfect."

1 c **2** c, d

Week 12, Day 2
Pg 63

Yesterday was Mom's birthday. Aunt Minnie sent Mom a pink, fluffy jacket. Mom hates pink, and she hates fluffy.

"I must ring her to say thank you," Mom said. "Aunt Minnie is a dear to remember my birthday, even if she doesn't remember what I like," Mom said.

"Aunt Minnie is family, and you can't choose your family. Mmmm ... perhaps I could wash it and say that it shrank."

1 Mom/her birthday

2 a "Aunt Minnie is a dear to remember my birthday, even if she doesn't remember what I like."

b "Perhaps I could wash it and say that it shrank."

Week 12, Day 3
Pg 64

1 Check for correct spelling of each word.

2 el: angel, novel, travel, panel, level, camel, tunnel, kennel, cruel, parcel, towel, label

le: handle, noodle, puddle, title, dimple

al: oval, total, signal

3 a noodle **b** parcel **c** handle **d** kennel

Week 12, Day 4
Pg 65

1 a parcal parcel **b** puddel puddle **c** towl towel **d** dimpl dimple **e** travl travel

2 Check for correct spelling of each word.

3 a buckle **b** shovel **c** cereal **d** people

4 a double **b** hospital **c** turtle

Week 12, Day 5
Pg 66

1 a . **b** ? **c** ? **d** . **e** ? **f** . **g** . **h** ?

2 *Answers will vary. Suggested answer:* Eddie is planting a flower.

3 *Answers will vary. Suggested answer:* I wonder what's inside this box?

Week 13, Day 1
Pg 67

A dog had a fresh, meaty bone, which a butcher had thrown to him. He was heading home with his wonderful bone, as fast as he could go.

1 a **2** b **3** b, d **4** d

Week 13, Day 2
Pg 68

As the dog crossed a bridge over a pond, he looked down and saw himself reflected in the quiet water. The image was like looking in a mirror.

But the dog thought he saw a real dog carrying another bone—a bone much bigger than his! Without thinking, the dog dropped his bone and leaped at the dog in the pond.

1 c

2 quiet, like looking in a mirror

3 d

4 *Answers will vary. Suggested answers:* mirrors, windows, shiny surfaces

5 the same

Week 13, Day 3
Pg 69

1 Check for correct spelling of each word.

2 a whorld world **b** whash wash **c** wite white **d** whorm worm **e** wich which

3 Missing letters are underlined

a world **b** witch **c** what **d** wheel/where **e** wipe **f** wall/want **g** wheel/where **h** went/well

Week 13, Day 4
Pg 70

1 a whale **b** wheat **c** worm **d** watch

2 Check for correct spelling of each word.

3 a whisk **b** wagon **c** wardrobe **d** whistle **e** weather

4 *Answers will vary. Suggested answers:* ward, robe, raw, row, rob, bored, draw, drew

Week 13, Day 5
Pg 71

1 a am **b** are **c** was **d** being **e** were

2 a is **b** was **c** are **d** am **e** were

3 a has **b** have **c** had

Week 14, Day 1
Pg 72

Berries to Jelly

Berries can be eaten fresh. They can also be cooked with sugar to make jelly.

1. Berries grow on small bushes or plants in fields and hothouses.
2. Some farmers use machines to harvest the ripe berries. Others are picked by hand.
3. The berries are washed, trimmed, and cut up or mashed. Then, the berries are cooked with sugar until the mixture is thick.
4. Next, the hot jelly is poured into jars and sealed to keep it fresh.

1 They are grown on small bushes or plants.

2 They are cooked with sugar until the mixture is thick.

3 into jars

4 the numbers next to each step

Week 14, Day 2
Pg 73

1 Then/Next/After this, Finally

2 *Suggested answer:* cows in shed, milking the cows, milk tanker, boiling the milk, milk in bottles, store

Week 14, Day 3
Pg 74

1 Check for correct spelling of each word.

2 a door **b** poor **c** after **d** even **e** hold

3 a sugar **b** hour **c** half **d** child

Week 14, Day 4
Pg 75

1 after, again, bath, child, climb, door, even, father, grass, great, half, hold, hour, past, poor, pretty, prove, sugar, sure, who

2 Check for correct spelling of each word.

3 a stek steak **b** butiful beautiful **c** wole whole **d** everibody everybody **e** cloes clothes

4 *Answers will vary. Read through sentence together.*

Week 14, Day 5
Pg 76

1 a is **b** am **c** has **d** are **e** have

2 *Answers will vary. Suggested answers:*
a riding his scooter.
b singing in the tree.

3 a have has **b** is are **c** was were

Week 15, Day 1
Pg 77

1 ✔ c, d, f ✘ a, b, e

2 pens and hammers

3 hammers, pens, and calculators

4 a calculator

5 a blender

Week 15, Day 2
Pg 78

1970s

Many new tools and gadgets became popular in the 1970s.

Prior to the 1970s, most schools used books, blackboards, and paper as educational tools.

By the 1970s, many schools had film projectors, record players and tape recorders to help children learn.

By the late 1970s, people began to buy personal computers for their homes.

1

School Tool	Used before 1970	Used in the 1970s	Used today
Books	✔	✔	✔
Blackboards	✔	✔	✘
Paper and pencils	✔	✔	✔
Film projectors	✘	✔	✘
Record players	✘	✔	✘
Tape recorders	✘	✔	✘

2 books, blackboards, paper, and pencils

3 books, paper, and pencils

Week 15, Day 3
Pg 79

1 Check for correct spelling of each word.

2 a olive, olives **b** leaf, leaves **c** hive, hives **d** scarf, scarves

3 a gloves **b** giraffes **c** shelves

Week 15, Day 4
Pg 80

1 just add s: puffs, safes, reefs, cliffs, waves, stoves, sleeves, hives, olives, gloves, cafes, giraffes
change f to ves: lives, wives, elves, leaves, wolves, loaves, scarves, shelves

2 Check for correct spelling of each word.

3 a knives **b** calves **c** grooves **d** halves

4 *Answers will vary. Read through sentence together.*

Week 15, Day 5
Pg 81

1 Present progressive: is picking, are jogging
Past progressive: was picking, were jogging

2 a am **b** is **c** am **d** are

3 a was **b** is **c** were **d** are

Week 16, Day 1
Pg 82

> **Transport**
> *Vehicles,* such as cars, buses, trains,
> planes, and boats, *transport us from*
> *one place to another.*
> Some people use transport to make
> short, daily trips to work or school.
> Others use it for longer journeys, such as
> a holiday or business trip overseas.
> Public transport is designed for moving
> large groups of people. Buses trains
> trams ferries and planes are types
> of public transport. Private transport
> includes cars, motorcycles, and bicycles.

1

	Purpose	Examples
Private transport	moving small numbers of people	cars, motorcycles and bicycles
Public transport	moving large groups of people	buses, trains, trams, ferries and planes

2 takes people from place to place

Week 16, Day 2
Pg 83

> **Cars**
> In the early 1900s people began to
> buy their own cars. In 1908, Henry
> Ford began making cars on an
> assembly line. His factory made cars
> at a much faster rate. These mass-
> produced cars were cheaper to buy.
> In the 1950s, many more people
> owned cars. More cars meant more
> roads. With more cars on the road,
> people started to think about car
> safety. The first seat belts strapped
> across the driver's lap.

1

Early 1900s	1908	1950s
People began to buy cars	First assembly line cars	First seatbelts

2 a **3** c

Week 16, Day 3
Pg 84

1 Check for correct spelling of each word.
2 a soup **b** fruit **c** shoe **d** suit
3 a ruby **b** shoe **c** fruit **d** prune
 e blue

Week 16, Day 4
Pg 85

1 Missing letters are <u>underlined</u>
 a sc<u>rew</u> **b** cl<u>ue</u> **c** g<u>rew</u>
 d c<u>rew</u> **e** b<u>lue</u>/b<u>lew</u> **f** f<u>lew</u>
 g ch<u>ew</u> **h** th<u>rew</u> **i** s<u>oup</u>
2 Check for correct spelling of each word.
3 a could **b** canoe **c** gruesome
 d through
4 a bruise **b** cashew **c** could
 d should

Week 16, Day 5
Pg 86

1 a up the tree/to the treehouse.
 b by bus.
 c at seven o'clock.
2 a will **b** is **c** am **d** going **e** to
3 a Tomorrow I will/am going to buy
 a new model plane.
 b Next week I will/am going to visit
 my cousins in Hawaii.

Week 17, Day 1
Pg 87

> Dear Mom,
> Today we got up really early and
> went to the zoo. It was huge! The
> giraffes had lots of room and
> the lions hid in the bushes. Dad
> pretended to be a mountain goat.
> We bought ice creams after lunch.
> Boo-boo had chocolate and I had
> vanilla. Dad carried us when we got
> really tired. See you tomorrow!
> Love, T
> xx

1 *Answers will vary. Check responses.*
2 *Answers will vary. Check responses.*

Week 17, Day 2
Pg 88

> Dear Anna and Janek,
> We arrived in Paris yesterday
> afternoon. Last night we went
> up to the top of the Eiffel Tower.
> The city was all lit up and so
> pretty. Today we went to three
> art galleries, so I have sore feet!
> What have you been doing?
> Love, Vicky and Sean

1 a card you write about your vacation
2 to tell their friends and family about
 their vacations
3 where they are, what they've seen,
 how they feel
4 *Answers will vary. Check postcard has
 a greeting, details of a vacation, and
 a sign-off.*

Week 17, Day 3
Pg 89

1 Check for correct spelling of each word.
2 ful: awful, helpful, spoonful, plateful,
 handful, thankful, forgetful, powerful,
 cheerful, joyful, playful, mouthful,
 graceful, grateful, spiteful, truthful
 less: useless, careless, restless,
 harmless

Week 17, Day 4
Pg 90

1 a <u>spoonfull</u> spoonful
 b <u>platefull</u> plateful
 c <u>careles</u> careless
 d <u>truthfull</u> truthful
2 Check for correct spelling of each word.
3 a plentiful **b** colorless **c** wonderful
 d disgraceful
4 *Answers will vary. Read through
 sentence together.*

Week 17, Day 5
Pg 91

1 you: yourself, he: himself, she: herself,
 it: itself, we: ourselves, you: yourselves,
 them: themselves
2 a himself **b** itself **c** themselves
 d ourselves **e** himself
3 a herself **b** themselves
 c ourselves **d** himself **e** yourself

Week 18, Day 1
Pg 92

1 a that live in the wild
b live in the water some of the time
2 a extreme **b** severe **c** low

Week 18, Day 2
Pg 93

1 easy to break
2 Handle with care and the pictures
3 the contents can be broken, handle with care
4 *Answers will vary. Suggested answers:* glass, crystal, porcelain
5 *Answers will vary. Suggested answer:* on a package of crystal glasses

Week 18, Day 3
Pg 94

1 Check for correct spelling of each word.
2 a gnome **b** knife **c** knot **d** write
3 a write **b** kneel **c** gnash

Week 18, Day 4
Pg 95

1 a knock **b** knelt **c** knot **d** wrist
2 Check for correct spelling of each word.
3 a knuckle **b** wriggle **c** knight
d wreckage **e** knead
4 *Answers will vary. Read through story together.*

Week 18, Day 5
Pg 96

1 a . **b** ! **c** ! **d** . **e** . **f** !/.
2 a How brilliant was that!
b How exciting is this!
3 a What a cute puppy that is!
b What an exciting ride that was!

REVIEW 2
Spelling
Pg 97

1 Missing letters are underlined
a towel **b** oval **c** puddle
2 c
3 Missing letters are underlined
a knob **b** wrist **c** whale
d gnash
4 a
5 a parties **b** rubies **c** scarves
d cafes

Grammar
Pg 98–99

1 a run **b** catch
2 a cook cooked **b** wash washed
3 a ? **b** .
4 a is **b** am **c** have
5 a am **b** are
6 a ~~were~~ was **b** ~~are~~ is
7 will **b** am
8 a themselves **b** herself
c yourself
9 a ! **b** .

Comprehension
100–101

1 b **2** c **3** a **4** c **5** b **6** d
7 c **8** a **9** d **10** b

Week 19, Day 1
Pg 102

Imagine This, Imagine That

"It's easy. One person starts imagining something that doesn't exist, say a flying car, and the next person has to add to it," said Lulu. "So, you could imagine a flying car shaped like a fish," said Aunt Stella. Sophie understood. "And the flying car shaped like a fish could spray fireworks from its wheels."

1 a **2** b **3** d

Week 19, Day 2
Pg 103

Art Eyes

"Look out for colours, patterns, shapes, textures, and shadows that catch your attention. Draw them in your journal and collect as much treasure as you can!" Aunt Stella cried.

Sophie liked the shapes and colors of the shells. She collected lots of shells of all shapes, sizes, colors, and patterns.

Sophie also rubbed some rock textures into her journal and drew a rough sketch of the beach. But her most precious find was a piece of blue, weathered glass.

1 shells
2 a sketch of the beach
3 precious
4 *Answers will vary. Suggested answer:* One day I found a beautiful peacock's feather. I took it home and put it in a jar. It's the most precious thing I have.

Week 19, Day 3
Pg 104

1 Check for correct spelling of each word.
2 est: finest, loudest, neatest, newest, coldest, thickest, fullest, smallest, clearest
er: paler, duller, nicer, fewer, later, cuter, whiter, fresher, prouder, steeper, sharper
3 a smalest smallest **b** coouter cuter
c steper steeper

Week 19, Day 4
Pg 105

1 a sharper **b** nicer **c** paler
d fresher **e** neatest
2 Check for correct spelling of each word.
3 a younger **b** brightest **c** straighter
d fiercer **e** higher
4 *Answers will vary. Read through sentences together.*

Week 19, Day 5
Pg 106

1 a cat **b** bird **c** Ruby **d** Liam
e baby **f** book **g** Sam **h** frog
i Mandy **j** monkey
2 Check: a, d, e
3 a Alex is wearing Jose's mitt.
b Dad's car is in the garage.
c My grandpa's glasses are on the table.
d The boy's lunch is in his bag.
e The child's T-shirt is covered in mud.
f Ben's kitten is very playful.

Week 20, Day 1
Pg 107

Smelly and Stuck

Jake's toenail went PING! Jake spun around like a corkscrew. And there he stuck.

Everybody pushed and shoved. People with cameras took photos. People with notebooks asked questions.

"What does it feel like to be trapped by your toenail, Jake? they asked.

The sacks were full of fertilizer. The longest toenail in the world was no fun anymore.

1 b **2** c **3** a **4** b

Week 20, Day 2
Pg 108

Sam's Cool Idea

The longest toenail in the world was growing.

Longer and wider and taller! And it was growing FAST!

It curled three times round his body. It shot past his ears. It twisted over his head. It snaked up past the diving board.

Jake gasped as his toenail snaked and grew. As big as himself ... as tall as a tree ... as big as a house ... as tall as a crane.

1 *Answers will vary. Suggested answer:* a drawing of a boy with a very long toenail.

2 *Answers will vary. Suggested answer:* I would feel excited to be different to everyone else.

3 Jake gasped

Week 20, Day 3
Pg 109

1 Check for correct spelling of each word.

2 a flea **b** hole **c** toe **d** plane **e** sail **f** rain **g** meat **h** steal

3 a plane **b** hole **c** sail **d** sale **e** steal

Week 20, Day 4
Pg 110

1 a flea **b** rein **c** steel **d** flee **e** prey

2 Check for correct spelling of each word.

3 a morning **b** rays **c** higher **d** Hall **e** where

4 *Answers will vary. Read through sentences together.*

Week 20, Day 5
Pg 111

1 a mine **b** our **c** her **d** your **e** my **f** their

2 a his **b** your **c** mine **d** ours **e** their

3 a my **b** its **c** theirs **d** mine

Week 21, Day 1
Pg 112

The Home Haircut

"Easy," said Jan as she cut. "Piece of cake!"

I remember when Jan said cooking was easy. We spent an afternoon scraping burned food off the stove.

Jan also told me that camping was easy. The tent fell on top of us during the night.

By three o'clock on Saturday afternoon there was more hair on the bathroom floor than on my head.

1 c **2** c **3** a

Week 21, Day 2
Pg 113

The Home Haircut

"Look in the mirror, Freya," said Jan.

I did. There was a lot of face and not much hair.

"Is it all right?" Jan said, looking worried.

"One side is longer than the other," I said softly.

Jan cut some more. Snip. Snip. Snip.

In the mirror, I looked strange. My hair was gone. Bits stuck out all over the place.

Jan's face was white.

1 she doesn't like it

2 she says, "I looked strange."

3 *Answers will vary. Suggested answer:* Drawing of Freya with short, uneven hair, and Jan looking very nervous.

Week 21, Day 3
Pg 114

1 Check for correct spelling of each word.

2 ing: jogging, wagging, stopping, bobbing, gripping, trapping

ed: rubbed, jogged, sagged, sipped, rammed, tipped, thinned, planned, stabbed, grabbed, stopped, blotted, skinned, flopped

3 a jogging **b** jogged **c** grabbed **d** bobbing

Week 21, Day 4
Pg 115

1 Check for correct spelling of each word.

2 a shipped **b** knitting **c** throbbed **d** stunned **e** squatted

3 a scanning **b** shrugged **c** scrubbing **d** strapping **e** prodding

Week 21, Day 5
Pg 116

1 a asked **b** replied **c** exclaimed **d** shrieked **e** sobbed **f** grumbled **g** yelled

2 a gasped **b** cheered **c** greeted **d** begged **e** warned **f** complained **g** whispered

Week 22, Day 1
Pg 117

Ringmaster Roy: Chuckles, perhaps you could teach Snoz about being a clown.

Narrator: Chuckles had a great time dressing Snoz and painting him with make-up. But when Snoz saw himself in the mirror, he hid under the table.

Snoz: Not funny! Too scary! Snoz is scared!

Narrator: Snoz began to cry. Seeing a Snozalot cry made Chuckles cry too.

Chuckles: (sobbing) That is the saddest thing I have ever seen. A sobbing Snozalot!

1 a

2 b, c

Week 22, Day 2
Pg 118

Ringmaster Roy: Tell me troupe, what can Snoz the Snozalot Monster do?

Chuckles: I will tell you what he cannot do. He cannot make you laugh.

Bendy Betty: He cannot bend.

Max Manyhands: He cannot juggle.

Ringmaster Roy: I see, I see. I see. And I know he can't fly though the air.

Chuckles: He's a nice monster.

Bendy Betty: A lovely monster, really.

Max Manyhands: But Snoz has no place in Circus Bizurkus.

1 Snoz the Snozalot Monster/Circus Bizurkus

2 a do circus acts.

b no place in Circus Bizurkus.

Week 22, Day 3
Pg 119

1 Check for correct spelling of each word.

2 a beak **b** rock **c** mask **d** trunk

3 ck words: lock, rock, tick, luck, peck, track, pluck, check, stick, shack, stock

k words: beak, bank, tank, pink, dusk, cheek, mask, speak, trunk

Week 22, Day 4
Pg 120

1 a bank **b** pink **c** dusk

2 Check for correct spelling of each word.

3 a cloak **b** stork **c** chipmunk **d** crook

4 a soak **b** thank **c** cloak **d** chipmunk

Week 22, Day 5
Pg 121

1 a "How many pets have you got?"
b "I'll wait for you outside,"
c "How good was that!"
d "Come here at once!"
e "I wish I had a pet hamster,"
f "Now, what have I done with my purse?"

2 a "How are you feeling today?" asked the doctor.
b "I would like oatmeal for breakfast," said the child.
c "What a large bear!" gasped Victoria.
d "Don't go too near the edge," warned the ranger.
e "I will never do that again," promised Ethan.

3 *Answers will vary. Suggested answer:* "I am 7 years old," said Adam.

Week 23, Day 1
Pg 122

The gnat dived at the lion and stung him on the nose. The lion was furious. He swiped at the gnat, but only ended up scratching himself with his sharp claws. The gnat attacked the lion again and again, and the lion raged.

1 d **2** a, e **3** d

Week 23, Day 2
Pg 123

Finally, the lion was worn out. He was dripping with blood from his own scratches and he lay down, defeated by the gnat. The gnat buzzed away to tell the whole Animal Kingdom about his victory over the lion, but instead he flew straight into a spider's web.

1 b

2 a defeated by the gnat
b worn out the lion

3 Don't be too quick to claim victory.

Week 23, Day 3
Pg 124

1 Check for correct spelling of each word.

2

quick	quickly
strong	strongly
most	mostly
nice	nicely

3 a easly easily **b** quikly quickly
c sofly softly **d** sudenly suddenly
e slowlee slowly

Week 23, Day 4
Pg 125

1 badly, calmly, clearly, easily, fairly, firmly, gently, happily, largely, mainly, mostly, nicely, quickly, quietly, shyly, slowly, softly, strongly, suddenly, swiftly

2 Check for correct spelling of each word.

3 a equally **b** finally **c** completely
d slightly

4 *Answers will vary. Read through sentence together.*

Week 23, Day 5
Pg 126

1 a bravely **b** brightly **c** equally
d sleepily **e** greedily **f** Gently

2 a loud loudly **b** healthy healthily
c loose loosely **d** beautiful beautifully
e careful carefully

3 *Answers will vary. Suggested answers:* correctly/clearly/incorrectly

Week 24, Day 1
Pg 127

Finding Fossils

Places where rocks are eroding might have fossils. Creek banks, dry riverbeds and cliff faces are all good places to look. Most fossils are covered by a thick layer of rock. At some sites, explosives blow up the rock and bulldozers cart it away. Often the whole block of rock, with its bones, is cut out. This is taken back to the lab where the bones are carefully removed.

1 5, 3, 2, 4, 6, 1

2 museum

Week 24, Day 2
Pg 128

Giant Jigsaw Puzzles

Putting a dinosaur back together takes skill, patience and a lot of time. Using photos and drawings, the skeleton is laid out on the floor and then put back together from the ground up. Most bones are too fragile to become a skeleton in a museum. A plaster or plastic cast is made. It is rare to find a complete skeleton—most museums' dinosaurs are put together with extra parts.

1 *Answers will vary. Suggested answer:* Drawings of the bones. Skeleton on the floor. Making a cast. Skeleton put together.

Week 24, Day 3
Pg 129

1 Check for correct spelling of each word.

2 a badge **b** orange **c** bridge
d hedge **e** judge

3 a smudge **b** strange **c** image
d orange **e** hedge

Week 24, Day 4
Pg 130

1 a plunge **b** change **c** fringe
d village **e** charge **f** garage

2 Check for correct spelling of each word.

3 a cottage **b** package **c** courage
d partridge **e** sausage

4 a damage **b** passage **c** package

Week 24, Day 5
Pg 131

1 a always **b** already **c** tomorrow **d** later/tomorrow **e** weekly/tomorrow

2 a hourly **b** regularly **c** never **d** earlier **e** now **f** sometimes **g** tonight

3 *Answers will vary. Suggested answer:* Yesterday I went to the beach.

Week 25, Day 1
Pg 132

A World-changing Gizmo

It all began in 1947. That's when three scientists invented the transistor. The three scientists were from the Bell Laboratories. Their names were John Bardeen, Walter Brattain, and William Shockley.

The first transistor was about the size of your thumb. It was made from a paperclip, gold foil, wire, and a bit of plastic. Transistors were first used in telephones.

Transistors are in computers, the Internet, cell phones, TVs, video cameras, calculators, hand-held games, radar, satellites, and night vision technology.

1 c

2 b

3 b

Week 25, Day 2
Pg 133

Why Didn't I Think of That?

Dr. Nakamatsu is a modern inventor. He holds the world record for the most patents and inventions. Dr. Nakamatsu has over 3,200 inventions.

Dr. Nakamatsu often came up with ideas underwater. He invented a notepad that he could use underwater to write down his ideas.

Dr. Nakamatsu only sleeps four hours a night. He says the best time for new ideas is between midnight and 4 a.m. He has two special rooms that help him think.

1 He had ideas underwater but couldn't write them down.

2 He invented a notepad that he could use underwater.

3 *Answers will vary. Read through answers together.*

Week 25, Day 3
Pg 134

1 Check for correct spelling of each word.

2 a starfish **b** hairbrush **c** raincoat **d** pancake

Week 25, Day 4
Pg 135

1 a Strawbery Strawberry
b snoman snowman
c raincote raincoat
d bakpack backpack
e harebrush hairbrush

2 Check for correct spelling of each word.

3 a watermelon **b** outside **c** marketplace **d** doughnut

4 a watermelon **b** clockwork

Week 25, Day 5
Pg 136

1 a barbecue **b** umbrella **c** candy **d** man **e** pickup **f** mice **g** day **h** bat **i** shape

2 a fluffy **b** juicy **c** electric **d** tiny **e** new **f** dirty

Week 26, Day 1
Pg 137

1

	Travels on and between					Travel for			Time …		On board		
	rivers	harbors	lakes	cities	countries	work	holiday	school	minutes or hours	days or weeks	shops	movie theaters	restrooms
ferry	✔	✔	✔	✔	✔	✔		✔	✔				✔
cruise ship				✔	✔		✔			✔	✔	✔	✔

2 restrooms

3 cities and countries

Week 26, Day 2
Pg 138

1

Boat	What does it do?	How many people	Interesting fact
destroyer	protects bigger, slower ships	300	moves fast
submarine	travels underwater	150	moves fast
aircraft carrier	carries planes	5,000	biggest ship in the Navy

2 They are all navy vessels.

Week 26, Day 3
Pg 139

1 Check for correct spelling of each word.

2 a h'es he's **b** cant' can't **c** she'l she'll **d** Im I'm **e** I'ts It's

3 a where's **b** didn't **c** I've **d** how's

Week 26, Day 4
Pg 140

1 a it'll **b** we'll **c** won't **d** you'd

2 Check for correct spelling of each word.

3 a weren't **b** would've **c** doesn't **d** wasn't **e** couldn't **f** you're

4 a wasn't **b** mustn't **c** couldn't **d** o'clock

Week 26, Day 5
Pg 141

1 a six **b** new **c** hungry **d** front **e** huge

2 a clearly **b** quickly **c** carefully **d** politely

3 a young beautifully **b** large fiercely **c** little brightly

Week 27, Day 1
Pg 142

Hoofed Mammals

Hoofed mammals eat plants. They are herbivores. Zebras, giraffes, and elephants are all hoofed mammals.

Many hoofed mammals live in groups called herds. They often live on open plains or grasslands. The herd moves from place to place in search of food. Zebras and wildebeests live in large herds.

Elephants are the largest land animals. They live in family groups called herds. Baby elephants feed on mother's milk for two years while they grow.

1 d

2 c

Week 27, Day 2
Pg 143

Monkeys and Apes

Monkeys and apes are mammals called primates. They are warm-blooded, furry animals that suckle their young.

Baboons, mandrills, and howlers are all monkeys. Monkeys are very good climbers. They use their hands, feet, and tails to help them climb.

Apes are larger than monkeys. Chimpanzees, gibbons, orangutans, and gorillas are all apes. Apes do not have tails.

Gorillas are the largest of all the apes and are tailless. They live in family groups.

1

small	larger	largest
Monkeys (baboons, mandrills, and howlers)	Apes (chimpanzees, gibbons, orangutans)	Gorillas

2 Monkeys have tails but apes don't.

3 "Apes do not have tails."

Week 27, Day 3
Pg 144

1 Check for correct spelling of each word.
2 **a** spider, spiders **b** bee, bees **c** dish, dishes **d** book, books **e** lion, lions **f** eye, eyes **g** shark, sharks **h** lamb, lambs

Week 27, Day 4
Pg 145

1 **a** pigs **b** lions **c** bees **d** coats **e** books **f** bunches
2 Check for correct spelling of each word.
3 **a** giraffes **b** flowers **c** fingers **d** oranges
4 **a** monkeys **b** fingers

Week 27, Day 5
Pg 146

1 **a** hasn't **b** can't **c** I've **d** isn't **e** aren't
2 **a** i **b** a **c** o **d** ha
3 **a** they'll **b** didn't **c** that's **d** haven't **e** doesn't

REVIEW 3
Spelling
Pg 147

1 **a** spiders **b** branches
2 c 3 **a** k **b** dge
4 **a** who's **b** would've
5 b 6 pancake
7 b 8 knitng knitting

Grammar
Pg 148–149

1 **a** Dan's **b** baby's
2 **a** (hers)(yours) **b** (Their)(mine)
3 **a** yelled **b** whispered
4 **a** "How many candies have you had?" asked Joey.
b "Not half as many as you," replied Ella.
5 **a** soft softly **b** tight tightly **c** quick quickly **d** heavy heavily
6 **a** later **b** immediately
7 **a** squirrels **b** table
8 little quickly **b** orange gently
9 **a** We'll **b** It's

Comprehension
Pg 150–151

1 d 2 b 3 b 4 b 5 c 6 c
7 a 8 b 9 c 10 b

Week 28, Day 1
Pg 152

The Sniffles
Vinnie raced in the front door. His bag skidded across the living room floor.
"What's going on in here?" Vinnie's mom stood in the doorway, hands on her hips.
Vinnie walked over and picked up his bag.
"Sorry, Mom. I'm in a bit of a hurry."
"What about a snack?"
"I'm not hungry."
Mary stood in shock as she watched him run up the stairs.

1 a 2 b, c 3 c

Week 28, Day 2
Pg 153

Dr. Hacker
Vinnie pulled the ad from his pocket and dialled the number.
"Hello," said the voice on the other end of the line.
"Are you Dr. Hacker?" asked Vinnie.
"That's right."
Vinnie explained his problem.
"Never fear, young Vinnie. I'll be there in a flash," said Dr. Hacker.
Vinnie hung up. Smoke filled the hall and a flash of light blinded him.
Dr. Hacker waved away the smoke.
"Show me your sick computer."

1 It's a computer problem.
2 He is magical.
3 The text says, "Smoke filled the hall and a flash of light blinded him."

Week 28, Day 3
Pg 154

1 Check for correct spelling of each word.
2 **a** became **b** bound **c** sprang **d** fought **e** swung **f** awoke
3 Missing letters are underlined
a did **b** clung **c** chose **d** froze **e** stole
4 **a** awake awoke **b** shake shook **c** eat ate **d** give gave **e** forget forgot

Week 28, Day 4
Pg 155

1 Check for correct spelling of each word.
2 **a** brought **b** taught **c** struck **d** understood **e** caught
3 **a** caught **b** shrank **c** brought **d** struck **e** taught **f** built

Week 28, Day 5
Pg 156

1 **a** thought **b** bought **c** fell **d** brought **e** went **f** felt
2 **a** gave **b** ate **c** was **d** won **e** stole **f** began **g** had
3 **a** knew **b** told **c** sat **d** wrote **e** flew **f** saw **g** made **h** taught

Week 29, Day 1
Pg 157

1 b, d
2 c

Week 29, Day 2
Pg 158

1 *Answers will vary. Read answers together.*
2 *Answers will vary. Read answers together.*
3 *Answers will vary. Discuss pictures together.*

Week 29, Day 3
Pg 159

1 Check for correct spelling of each word.
2 **a** smile **b** plate **c** bone **d** nine
3 **a** bone **b** smile **c** plate **d** stone **e** blade **f** nine
4

a–e	e–e	i–e	o–e	u–e
face	these	nine	bone	June
safe		smile	close	rule
plate		glide	stone	prune
skate		slide	alone	
blade			stole	
shade			whole	

Week 29, Day 4
Pg 160

1 Check for correct spelling of each word.
2 **a** crocodile **b** lemonade **c** tadpole **d** whale **e** microwave
3 **a** scrape **b** shave **c** tadpole **d** gnome

Week 29, Day 5
Pg 161

1 a to **b** out **c** past **d** beside
e with **f** of **g** in

2 a at **b** past **c** above **d** on
e under **f** for **g** in

3 a *Answers will vary. Suggested answer:* on, in, on

Week 30, Day 1
Pg 162

A man just one
also a fly just one
in the huge drawing room
Kobayashi Issa

1 a, d **2** b, d **3** b **4** b

Week 30, Day 2
Pg 163

Warm snug speckled egg
Dappled light fading quickly
Soft crack of split shell
Alysha Hodge

1 d **2** d **3** c **4** d

Week 30, Day 3
Pg 164

1 Check for correct spelling of each word.

2 ee words: meet, feet, greet, fleet, sheet, sweet, tweet, street
ea words: meat, heat, seat, beat, neat, treat, cheat, pleat, wheat, bleat, upbeat, repeat

3 a greet **b** sheet **c** feet **d** street

Week 30, Day 4
Pg 165

1 a fleet **b** bleat **c** beat **d** tweet
e wheat

2 Check for correct spelling of each word.

3 a overeat **b** retreat **c** athlete
d parakeet

4 a compete **b** complete **c** heartbeat

Week 30, Day 5
Pg 166

1 a against **b** in **c** since **d** with

2 a when **b** where **c** how **d** when
e how

3 a at **b** by **c** to **d** in

Week 31, Day 1
Pg 167

A hungry fox was looking for food. She saw bunches of juicy, plump grapes growing high up on a farmer's fence.

"I will have those grapes. I'm starving!" she said.

1 d **2** b, d **3** b

Week 31, Day 2
Pg 168

The fox ran at the fence and leaped as high as she could. It was a great leap—but it wasn't high enough. She hadn't even reached the lowest bunch of grapes.

The fox tried again. She ran and leaped and it was another wonderful leap. But once again, she did not jump high enough to reach the fruit. She didn't give up though.

1 b

2 a but it wasn't high enough
b again but it wasn't high enough

Week 31, Day 3
Pg 169

1 Check for correct spelling of each word.
a tractor **b** saucer **c** doctor **d** spider

3 a dinner **b** cracker **c** brother **d** saucer
e finger **f** tractor

4 a enter **b** together **c** mirror
d another **e** wander **f** pepper

Week 31, Day 4
Pg 170

1 a docter doctor **b** peppor pepper
c doller dollar **d** mirrar mirror
e wandor wander

2 Check for correct spelling of each word.

3 a alligator **b** September **c** November
d feather

4 *Answers will vary. Read through story together.*

Week 31, Day 5
Pg 171

1 Check: a, d, e

2 *Answers will vary. Read through sentences.*

3 a Are they having lunch?
b Is the monkey swinging in the tree?

Week 32, Day 1
Pg 172

Bengal Tigers

Some Bengal tigers live in the mangrove forests of India and Bangladesh.

Tigers hunt mammals, such as wild boars. Bengal tigers also eat saltwater crabs and fish.

Tigers are quick and powerful hunters. They have soft foot pads that help them quietly stalk prey. Their striped coats help them hide in the forest. Every tiger has a different pattern of stripes.

1 d

2 a, b, d

3 Drawing of a wild boar, crab, and fish.

Week 32, Day 2
Pg 173

Hippopotamuses

Hippos live in swampy lakes and rivers in Africa.

Hippos spend the day in the water. A hippo's eyes, ears, and nostrils are on the top of its head. It can watch for danger while the rest of its body is underwater.

Hippos nurse their young and even sleep underwater. Hippos do not truly swim. They run or walk along the river bed.

Hippos are often aggressive. They open their mouths to warn off intruders.

1 Drawing of a labeled hippopotamus

Week 32, Day 3
Pg 174

1 Check for correct spelling of each word.

2 a maid **b** decade **c** spade **d** aid
e raid

3 Missing letters are underlined
a invade **b** blade **c** wade
d sunshade **e** trade **f** arcade

4 afraid, aid, arcade, blade, decade, fade, grade, invade, laid, made, maid, paid, parade, raid, shade, spade, sunshade, trade, upgrade, wade

Week 32, Day 4
Pg 175

1 Check for correct spelling of each word.

2 a braid **b** marmalade **c** bridesmaid
d lemonade **e** persuade

3 a cascade **b** grenade **c** persuade

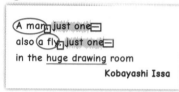

Week 32, Day 5
Pg 176

1 a . **b** ? **c** ! **d** . **e** ?
2 Check: a, c, e
3 a I have a dog and a cat.
b How old are you today?

Week 33, Day 1
Pg 177

1

Vegetable	Cooler weather	Warmer weather	Quick to grow	Longer to grow
carrot	✔			✔
corn		✔		✔
peppers		✔	✔	
onion	✔			✔
winter lettuce	✔		✔	
tomato		✔		✔

2 c, d, e

Week 33, Day 2
Pg 178

Cows and Sheep
Some farmers raise large herds of cattle. Others raise large flocks of sheep.
Farmers raise herds of cows, called cattle, for their meat and hides. Leather is made into shoes, clothes, and furniture. Cattle eat grass in fields or are fed hay and grain.
Dairy cows make milk. Milk can be made into cheese, yogurt, and ice cream.
Farmers raise sheep for their wool, meat, and milk. Farmers shear sheep once a year. The wool can be made into sweaters, blankets, and carpets.

1

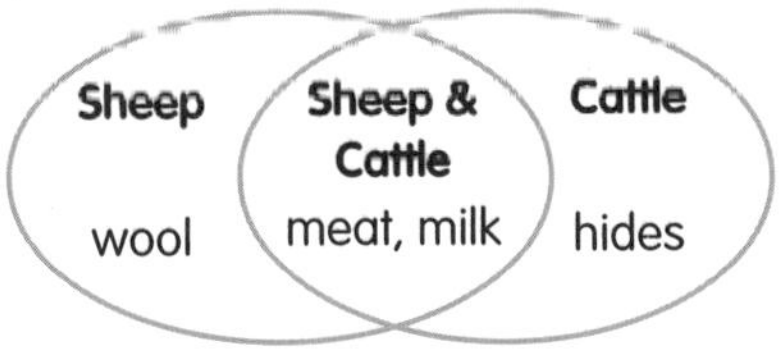

Week 33, Day 3
Pg 179

1 Check for correct spelling of each word.

2

happy	watch	begin
happiness	watching	beginning
happily	watched	beginner
happiest	watchful	began

3 a law **b** unlawful **c** fright **d** frightened
e watching

Week 33, Day 4
Pg 180

1 a watched **b** watchful **c** happiness
d beginning **e** beginner **f** fright
2 Check for correct spelling of each word.
3 a garden **b** deciding **c** gardener
d friendly **e** decide
4 *Answers will vary. Read through story together.*

Week 33, Day 5
Pg 181

1 a or **b** and **c** so **d** because **e** but
2 a and **b** until **c** because **d** so
e or, but
3 *Answers will vary. Suggested answer:*
a I like apples and I like watermelon.
b I looked under my bed, but I couldn't find my shoes.
c I dropped the box because I saw a mouse.

Week 34, Day 1
Pg 182

How a jet engine works
Jet engines burn a mixture of fuel and air. This makes hot gases, which give thrust. Thrust gets a plane off the ground and keeps it moving.

1 b **2** 3, 4, 1, 5, 2

Week 34, Day 2
Pg 183

Swing Wings
Wide wings help get a plane off the ground. They also slow it down in the sky. Swing wings solve this problem. On fighters like the F-14 Tomcat, the wings sweep back once the jet is in the air.

1 the wide wings
2 out to the sides
3 after take-off
4 they swing out to the sides again

Week 34, Day 3
Pg 184

1 Check for correct spelling of each word.
2 er: bigger, tinier, easier, heavier, happier, healthier, angrier, flatter, funnier
est: biggest, fattest, tiniest, easiest, saddest, heaviest, happiest, healthiest, angriest, busiest, funniest

Week 34, Day 4
Pg 185

1 a bigger **b** funniest **c** biggest
d easiest **e** happiest
2 Check for correct spelling of each word.
3 a fluffier/dirtier **b** dimmer
c curliest/dirtiest **d** tidier/dirtier
4 a smelliest **b** scariest **c** thinnest

Week 34, Day 5
Pg 186

1 a and **b** so **c** and **d** or **e** but
2 a fed, and, bathed **b** packed, but, left
c was, so, stayed **d** Drink, or, put
3 a Max plays basketball and Abby plays baseball.
b Jackson is tall, but Joshua is taller.

Week 35, Day 1
Pg 187

Healthy Foods
Your body needs a variety of good foods to grow and stay healthy.
The food we eat is called our diet. A balanced diet contains a wide variety of foods.
Carbohydrates in foods such as bread and rice give us energy. Other foods, like fruits and vegetables, are full of vitamins and minerals.
We need protein to make muscles, skin, and hair. Meat and eggs are high-protein foods. We need calcium for our teeth and bones. Dairy foods, like cheese and milk are high in calcium.

1

	Why we need them	Examples
Carbohydrates	give us energy	bread, rice
Fruit and vegetables	full of vitamins and minerals	*Answers will vary*
Protein	makes muscles, skin, and hair	eggs, meat
Dairy	good for teeth and bones	milk, cheese

Week 35, Day 2
Pg 188

> **Grains**
>
> A healthy diet should include grains, such as wheat, rice, and corn.
>
> Some grain is cooked and eaten whole. These are wholegrain foods. Other grain is ground into flour to make bread, pasta, and cereals. All grains have carbohydrates, which give the body energy.
>
> Some wholegrain foods are corn on the cob, rice, and wholegrain bread. They are high in fiber. Wholegrains contain magnesium, a mineral that helps build strong bones and teeth.

1 carbohydrates which the body can use for energy
2 fiber and magnesium
3 building strong bones and teeth

Week 35, Day 3
Pg 189

1 Check for correct spelling of each word.
2 a school **b** outside **c** mother **d** father
3 a off **b** wanted **c** pretty **d** with **e** outside **f** always
4 a have **b** off **c** around **d** next

Week 35, Day 4
Pg 190

1 a le l **b** outsde outside **c** wantid wanted **d** weth with **e** agein again
2 Check for correct spelling of each word.
3 a children **b** swimming **c** February **d** favorite **e** scared
4 *Answers will vary. Read through sentence together.*

Week 35, Day 5
Pg 191

1 a amazon **b** everest **c** thanksgiving **d** apple **e** pittsburg **f** canada
2 a grand canyon, arizona **b** ford, toyota **c** ravenscliff elementary school **d** saint patrick's day **e** europe, africa, south america
3 My best friend lives in Simpson Street.

Week 36, Day 1
Pg 192

> **1800s**
>
> *During the 1800s, machinery for making clothes was invented. More factories were built. Textiles became mass-produced.*
>
> Before machinery, weavers, and tailors made clothes by hand.
>
> Sewing machines were invented and then mass-produced during the 1800s. This allowed women at home to make clothing quickly and easily. Clothes of the 1800s were often uncomfortable to wear. Women wore bone corsets that laced up tightly.

1 a **2** b, e

Week 36, Day 2
Pg 193

> **1990s**
>
> *During the 1990s, people wore shirts, hats, and sunglasses to protect against skin cancer.*
>
> Hats were not popular in the 1970s and 1980s. In the 1990s, people became more aware of skin cancer. Hats became common again.
>
> Many bathing suits, especially for young children, once again covered much of the body. This was to protect them from the sun.

1 *Answers will vary. Suggested answers:* A drawing of people in the 1970s at the beach without a hat and a drawing of people in the 1990s wearing long sleeved bathing suits.

Week 36, Day 3
Pg 194

1 Check for correct spelling of each word.
2 Missing letters are underlined
a fitness **b** enjoyment **c** softness **d** thickness **e** blackness **f** darkness
3 a payment **b** treatment **c** fairness **d** movement **e** amusement **f** amazement
4 a sadnes sadness **b** darknes darkness **c** amazment amazement

Week 36, Day 4
Pg 195

1 Check for correct spelling of each word.
2 a argument **b** punishment **c** equipment **d** excitement
3 a willingness **b** astonishment **c** entertainment

Week 36, Day 5
Pg 196

1 a thanks **b** won't **c** yeah **d** movies **e** dunno **f** kid
2 a everybody **b** very good **c** delicious **d** would have **e** What is the matter? **f** quite soon
3 I have never been to Washington D.C.

REVIEW 4
Spelling
Pg 197

1 Missing letters are underlined
a skate **b** smile **c** sheet **d** afraid
2 b
3 a happily **b** happiness **c** happiest
4 Missing letters are underlined
a saucer **b** dollar **c** finger **d** tractor
5 d
6 allways always

Grammar
Pg 198–199

1 a ate **b** drank **c** brought
2 a around **b** in
3 a with **b** in
4 a sat **b** dug
5 a She has lost her keys. **b** What are they doing?
6 a because **b** but **c** so **d** or
7 Becky has a white cat, and Lucy has a black cat.
8 a independence day, miami **b** walmart
9 a Good morning **b** How are you?

Comprehension
200–201

1 b **2** a **3** d **4** a **5** d **6** a
7 b **8** d **9** b **10** c

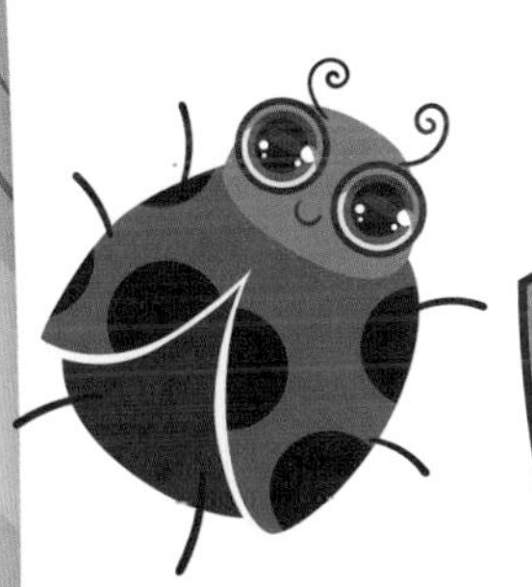

WELL DONE!

This is to certify

---

has completed the

Reading Eggspress

Grade 2

Program.

Date

Signature

Reading Eggs *Reading for Second Grade*
ISBN: 978-1-74215-343-8

Reprinted 2022

Published by:
Blake eLearning USA
37 West 26th Street,
Suite 201
New York, NY 10010

www.readingeggspress.com

Publisher: Katy Pike
Series writer: Laura Anderson
Series editor: Amy Russo
Editors: Alysha Hodge, Megan Smith

Designed and typeset by The Modern Art Production Group
Printed in China by 1010 Printing International Ltd.

The following extracts are reproduced with permission from the publisher, Blake Publishing and Blake Education.

Week 1 *Go, Go Gecko,* Bren MacDibble, Blake Education, 2010. **Week 2** *Tim's Money Tree*, Jan Weeks, Blake Education, 2010. **Week 3** *Songbird,* Claire Kamber, Blake Education, 2010. **Week 4** *Miss Feline's Unusual Pets*, Lisa Thompson, Blake Education, 2010. **Week 5** *The Ant and the Dove,* retold by Mark Stafford, Blake Education, 2011. **Week 6** *Summer*, Katy Pike, Blake Education, 2003. **Week 7** *Dry,* Liz Flaherty, Blake Education, 2009. **Week 8** *Trains*, Ian Rohr, Blake Education, 2003. **Week 9** *Bread,* Liz Flaherty, Blake Education, 2009. **Week 10** *Take Me to Your Leader,* Bren MacDibble, Blake Education, 2002. **Week 11** *Mandy Made Me Do It*, Jan Weeks, Blake Education, 2000. **Week 12** *Saving Greedy Guts,* Wendy Blaxland, Blake Education, 2002. **Week 13** *The Dog and his Reflection,* retold by Mark Stafford, Blake Education, 2011. **Week 14** *From Farms to You*, Paul McEvoy, Blake Education, 2003. **Week 15** *Tools,* Ian Rohr, Katy Pike and Laura Sieveking, Blake Education, 2009. **Week 16** *Transport*, Ian Rohr, Katy Pike and Laura Sieveking, Blake Education, 2009. **Week 17** *Postcards,* Mark Stafford, Blake Education, 2011. **Week 18** *Signs*, Mark Stafford, Blake Education, 2011. **Week 19** *Artrageous,* Lisa Thompson, Blake Education, 2005. **Week 20** *The World's Longest Toenail*, Susan Knight, Blake Education, 2002. **Week 21** *A Hairy Question,* Hazel Edwards, Blake Education, 2000. **Week 22** *Can I Join the Circus?*, Lisa Thompson, Blake Education, 2009. **Week 23** *The Lion and the Gnat,* retold by Mark Stafford, Blake Education, 2011. **Week 24** *Dinosaur Dig*, Ian Rohr, Blake Education, 2004. **Week 25** *Inventing the Future,* Lisa Thompson, Blake Education, 2005. **Week 26** *Boats*, Ian Rohr, Blake Education, 2003. **Week 27** *Mammals*, Paul McEvoy, Blake Education, 2002. **Week 28** *Computer Virus*, Christopher Stitt, Blake Education, 2003. **Week 29** *Game Plan,* Lisa Thompson, Blake Education, 2005. **Week 30** *Haiku*, Mark Stafford (Ed.), Blake Education, 2011. **Week 31** *The Fox and the Grapes,* retold by Mark Stafford, Blake Education, 2011. **Week 32** *Wet,* Liz Flaherty, Blake Education, 2009. **Week 33** *Farms*, Paul McEvoy, Blake Education, 2003. **Week 34** *Fighter Planes*, Ian Rohr, Blake Education, 2005. **Week 35** *Healthy Eating,* Paul McEvoy, Blake Education, 2003. **Week 36** *Clothes*, Ian Rohr, Katy Pike and Laura Sieveking, Blake Education, 2009.